THE LABOR OF ARCHITECTURE

The Labor of ARCHITECTURE

Creativity, Design, and the Building of a New Class Consciousness

by C. G. BECK

MONTHLY REVIEW PRESS
New York

Copyright © 2025 by C. G. Beck
All Rights Reserved

Library of Congress Cataloging-in-Publication data available from the publisher.

ISBN 978-168590-137-0 paper
ISBN 978-168590-139-4 cloth

Cover image: Thomas Hart Benton (1889–1975): "City Building," one of ten panels comprising the room-sized mural, "America Today" (1930–1931). Photo credit: © The Metropolitan Museum of Art; Image source: © ARS, NY, Art Resource, NY.

Typeset in Bulmer MT

MONTHLY REVIEW PRESS | NEW YORK
www.monthlyreview.org

5 4 3 2 1

Contents

Acknowledgments | 7
Preface | 10
Introduction | 19

Part One: Creative Consciousness | 42
Part Two: Class Consciousness | 84
Part Three: Together We Build | 110

Conclusion: What Is the Architecture of Labor? | 139
Selected Bibliography | 148
Notes | 151
Index | 174

Acknowledgments

This work began as a collective effort. I wrote the text in the plural because it was only possible through the joint effort of many, and most importantly the founding members of BA Union: Po-Yu, Emma, Stephanie, Sara, Prax, Irshaad, Brandon, Paul, Ayman, Armaan, Caleb, and Lauren. I also acknowledge the hours of thankless work of the Bargaining Committee: Kolby, Ann, and Je; a grind in the true sense of the word, with their day-by-day resilience and dedication a continued source of inspiration for effecting change in the messy realities of the world. And for the unwavering support of our lead organizer, negotiator, and visionary behind our growing movement, David DiMaria, not one for attention or praise, but who deserves plenty of it. For someone who knew nothing about architecture when he started this work, he's had a tremendous impact on our discipline.

I am indebted to the excellent team at Monthly Review Press: Martin Paddio, Rebecca Manski, and Erin Clermont for the careful review and steady hand in guiding the completion of this work. It's been an honor to work on this book with the same press that published Harry Braverman's seminal *Labor and Monopoly Capital*, a central source of research and inspiration. In particular, I want to thank Michael Yates, longtime editor at *Monthly Review*, whom I owe for taking a risk on this work by a first-time author. His patience, critical eye, and deep experience in the labor movement were fundamental in making this the best book it could possibly be.

Many thanks to Andy Bernheimer, founding principal of Bernheimer Architecture, not only for the professional support and career opportunities, but for a spirit that is the best of its kind in our industry. Though we've had our fair share of disagreements, we certainly see things in common more often than not. I was hired at BA in 2018 with the explicit directive that he and his office valued such productive disagreements, and we can see the fruits of that ethos today. Andy also deserves credit for being an advocate for labor in the architecture industry, a rare example of management doing so, unfortunately, but one I hope other owners in architecture and beyond find inspiration from.

The rare opportunity to study philosophy at the New School for Social Research while practicing as an architect has been instrumental in testing and refining many of the ideas found throughout this book, pushing me far beyond my comfort zone, and the final piece of the puzzle that allowed for a most productive critique of my discipline. Specifically, I thank Professors Dmitri Nikulin, Cinzia Arruzza, and Alice Crary, whose classes full of critical thinking and debate are reflected throughout this book. Most important, I want to thank Nancy Fraser, who provided an unending source of research related to the idea of "class," an unparalleled, lucid teaching of them, and continued support in my efforts to integrate this work with my own disciplinary background. We all owe her and the intellectual comrades in her generation for keeping alive many ideas that have long been dormant but are once again reemerging. I also want to acknowledge the students who have been a part of my classes at Parsons. Whether they realized it or not, their willingness to take risks and jump into unfamiliar territory helped shape much of my thinking here.

And finally, to the three women whose labor has built the foundation for much of this work: my sister Jen, whose brilliant scholarship has always been something I've looked up to; my mother, Leslie, whose devotion as an art teacher sparked a lifelong passion for art and creativity; and of course, my wife, Heather, whose love and faith in me was at times the only momentum I had while trying to navigate this discipline. From the volunteer work that brought us together, to our precarious life in graduate school, to licensure and now unionization. "Just write the damn book" was the best advice I didn't know I needed, and her support and encouragement in seeing things through is beyond special. I am forever grateful.

Preface

When I first encountered architecture in the early aughts, the discipline still viewed itself as "the mother of all arts," a dramatic expression of identity given to us by America's most famous architect, Frank Lloyd Wright. The sentiment appealed to me, so, uninterested in the typical topics found in secondary level education, I applied to a large state university's architecture program. Tepidly interested in the humanities and fine arts thanks to my mother, who was an art teacher, I was able to compile a portfolio for admittance to the more rigorous architecture studio sequence after managing general requirements.

Beginning my first fall semester in studio, I was instantly hooked. Neglecting past friendships, ACC basketball games, and sometimes even food and sleep, I dove all-in, consuming any and everything associated with architecture. I kept a sketch book and drew whenever I could, went to every visiting architect's lecture in our building, studied the "masters" by buying whatever architecture monographs I could afford, and completed the bare minimum for my non-architectural course work so I could get back to my studio desk as soon as possible. My new cohort and I were at our desks for what seemed like all hours of the day and night, debating new concepts we encountered, and critiquing each other's work. I had never experienced education like this before, and it was exhilarating. I shouldn't have been surprised, though—I had found a discipline that combined the freedom and experimentation of the fine arts with the pragmatic problem solving of design, all through an intensely rigorous and extraordinarily collaborative atmosphere, and I had never been so passionate about learning before. I had found what felt like purpose, and the future felt bright.

I would soon discover the broader context of this monastic-artistic existence, however. Before the studio sequence, when I was completing my general requirements, some of which included introductory architecture courses, the director of the program mentioned that "everyone in our program gets a job." While I was not necessarily eager to join the workforce, it was comforting to know that I had chosen a major that I loved, but that I also had good job prospects waiting at its culmination. It almost felt like I had discovered a secret formula, especially compared to other majors.

Then, in the fall of 2008, just one month into my first semester in studio, the stock market crashed. It was a strange experience, but as a junior in college I was fairly sheltered from the market—or so I thought. I knew things were bad based on the reaction of newspapers and pundits, but the immediate impacts were hard to discern. Pretending to understand the consequences of such a historic day, I went about life as usual, too distracted by my newfound passion to do much else but put my head down and work.

The reality of this cataclysmic shock to our economy became evident during the architecture department's annual career fair. Based on years past, I hesitantly attended, expecting a summer job offer like most students were, knowing it was an important step in our developing career paths. At the fair I made connections and had pleasant conversations, but the atmosphere was bleak, an underlying sense of tension and anxiety percolating throughout our grand atrium. It was only natural, as architecture is inextricably linked to the housing market, and this particular stock market crash was driven by subprime mortgages and risky derivative swaps, things I would later understand as fundamental to the growth of real estate and housing, and hence architecture. For a cohort of over fifty students, a small fraction were given tentative offers for internships, and I had my first economic crisis as an adult: what would I do that summer if I couldn't get work at an architect's office? Would I start falling behind? Miss out on skills and connections for future full-time jobs? Lose the vocation I had finally discovered? These were questions I had never wrestled with before, and though I found a gig as a sailing camp director, I knew I would eventually have to face facts. More important, these existential questions marked the beginning of an awareness that architecture wasn't a discipline solely concerned with creativity or artistry. It was a profession subject to the vicissitudes of our economic system, one that experienced periodic waves of instability and crisis. In other words, it was just like every other job.

A decade later, just before our next crisis arrived in the United States, this time in the form of a global pandemic, my relationship to a discipline that I once viewed as filled with purpose had significantly soured. With a stint in AmeriCorps and graduate school long behind me, I had been working in the private sector in New York City for several years. Having been laid off after one year at my first job—a typical occurrence for workers in architecture even during strong economies—I hopped around offices until landing at a medium-sized firm that had recently begun specializing in affordable housing. Initially I was excited again, eager to break away from the rich clients whose capricious desires plagued many offices, instead pursuing altruistic work akin to my time with AmeriCorps in New Orleans rebuilding homes devastated by Hurricane Katrina. I had long lost interest in the masters of my formative years, those architects who delivered specialty projects that adorned magazines and newspapers, but at a high cost that I had come to understand more clearly. Through after-work happy hours with former classmates and colleagues, grievance-filled conversations exposed the underlying realities that made such ostensibly compelling work possible: exploitation. I wanted no part of it anymore.

While my new office engaged in work that I found ethically admirable, giving me a certain level of assurance, many of my colleagues at other firms were not so lucky. I previously had worked at offices with similar ethos, built on low wages (especially for professionals), an expectation to be in the office long past the standard 9-to-5, and an overall relentless churn of fast-paced work that consumed what felt like all parts of each week. With the demand to work unpaid overtime at night and on weekends on very short notice for regular deadlines and attend "enriching" architecture events in our spare time (events that culturally placated such an existence), this felt less like a career and more like an all-consuming life project, but one lacking the creative agency of my education. Stripped of these artistic pursuits and rich self-development, we felt more like cogs, occasionally doing a bit of interesting work but mostly grinding away at our desks at the whims of others.

With the arrival of the COVID-19 pandemic, what felt like an inescapable system had suddenly started to show considerable weaknesses. For those of us who were fortunate enough to maintain our health and had the ability to work from home, we were afforded space from a daily cycle whose alternative was unimaginable. With this new time for contemplation, I took up a daunting project that had been on my list for some time: reading through the entirety of Marx's *Capital*, Volume I. With the upheaval of politics as usual in the U.S., I had begun to read such texts intermittently before the pandemic, but I never had the physical or mental space to engage deeply with such challenging ideas. Diligently reading each chapter with the help of online lectures, I was astounded at the universality of Marx's insights into our working conditions under capitalism. Though I had found the political predictions in other texts, theoretically known as "historical materialism," less convincing, the sociological insights of actual conditions at the center of *Capital* made Marx a deeply insightful critic for the contemporary problems I was wrestling with. While nineteenth-century factory workers faced much more pressing concerns regarding health and safety, there were new concepts I encountered that still felt universal to all workers: the inescapability of the working day, the production and confiscation of surplus-value, and the oppressiveness of technology, to name a few. What I came to understand was that we architects had not just been experiencing issues of a loss of creative agency, or a momentary slide along the path toward inevitable success, but the effects of the relations that structured all of these issues: an entrenched form of *class conflict*. This force, one that worked behind the scenes, was present not only in our discipline, but our entire economy, and my growing awareness of these kinds of cross-societal connections permanently changed how I viewed architecture.

Previously, like most Americans, I had understood class in purely economic terms: lower class, middle class, and upper class. While useful, this definition is narrow and only describes income, something that fluctuates over both space and time. At most I could surmise that architecture had historically been a middle-class, and occasionally upper-class, profession but had been slipping toward the lower end of the spectrum for some time, especially evident in my generation. Faced with a historic economic crisis at the beginning of our careers, one that entailed diminished job prospects, lower pay, and ballooning student debt, the discipline was significantly weakened. However, the "economic" conceptualization of class could only answer questions about *what*, but not *how* or *why*. In his work prior to *Capital*, which served as its foundation, Marx had importantly acknowledged that yes, these are useful categorizations, but they are "idealistic" and fail to speak to the underlying *social relations*, which are both determinant of, and determined by, such economic conditions. Most simply, this begins not with a three-way division of class, but a binary division, between those who *sell* their labor and those who *buy* it, or between workers and owners. From this starting point, the profession of architecture began to look very different, not as a dispersed group of "temporarily embarrassed" firm owners, in the words of John Steinbeck, but a potentially powerful collective of *workers*. Needless to say, the insights and applications from this thought process felt endless compared to the confined ways of thinking I was accustomed to. Architecture and design more broadly simply did not have the conceptual frameworks to engage with thinking at this scale. Finishing *Capital*, I began to work on a study project with the instinct that it was important to look outside of the discipline, a valuable lesson I first learned from the summer I spent sailing instead of working in an office. In other words, the answers to our most pressing questions were not found within architecture itself, but elsewhere.

This all occurred at the same time a nascent but historic labor movement was growing within architecture. Collectively frustrated with the issues mentioned above, workers began to see themselves as just that, workers, in line with Marx's definition of class, whether they knew it or not. After a failed campaign at a large office in New York, the workers at my office began the process of doing something unimaginable when I was an undergraduate student: organizing for unionization.

A second crucial opportunity was afforded me when I began teaching at Parsons, the New School, shortly after the beginning of the pandemic. Though employment at the college had generally eroded through decades of neoliberal austerity policies at the hands of corporate managers, working as an adjunct faculty had one excellent perk: the ability to take courses for free, thanks to our well-established union.[1] While continuing to work full-time as an architect, I began taking graduate courses at the New School for Social Research (another school within the broader university) focusing on philosophy and capitalism studies, seeking an intellectual atmosphere to foster the ideas I had begun exploring on my own.

Although I had no previous training in the humanities, I found a home in the philosophy department, a rigorous environment to bring ideas from architecture and design into an unfamiliar setting. And more important, I was exposed to new authors and ideas I never would have been before. The culmination of this process was a course taught by political philosopher Nancy Fraser called "Rethinking Class." Building off the definitions above, we dove further into the depths of the thorny problem of class, both in terms of its history in regard to labor movements, but also its contemporary neglect of race and gender. Here was an opportunity to really unite theory and praxis, bringing my experiences in organizing the first contemporary private-sector architecture union in the United States to an academic setting. My fellow classmates and I collectively wrestled with the relations of class to architects and designers, among other things. Professor Fraser's unparalleled teaching on the topics in this course and ongoing mentorship have been instrumental in the writing of this book.

Through these experiences, my understanding of class and my profession has been radically transformed. Perhaps this change is best summarized by Harry Braverman, a longtime director of Monthly Review Press, who, seeing through capital's increasing tendency to infiltrate all that orbits around it, was less concerned about distinctions between "productive and unproductive" labor, or categorical terms like "technical" or "professional," terms that hide an underlying structural reality: "The inclusion of draftsmen, medical, dental, engineering and other such technicians among the professional and technical grouping also, in a large and increasing number of cases, *conceals a genuinely working-class situation for those involved.*"[2] This book is centered around those in an "increasing number of cases." In other words, what makes certain jobs *different* from others is less important today than the social relations and qualities that *unite* workers across industries in contemporary capitalism. With ever-increasing specialization and technological change, the work of understanding the nuances of our individual disciplines is a necessary first step in order to determine what unites them, a prerequisite for universal participation in larger social movements and real change.

A FEW NOTES ON THE structure of this book. While the labor movement has a strong international presence, this work is specific to design-based class consciousness in the United States. Our particular history in relation to the emergence of New Deal–era labor reforms and our present lingering malaise as a result of the advanced neoliberalism of the 1980s and 1990s have created a very particular kind of consciousness, and though the origins are global, the effects are local. Further, I cannot claim to be an expert on the architectural labor movement outside of the United States, as my experience is very much rooted within it.

Of course, the changing economic circumstances of today's workers in design professions have also greatly contributed to the emergence of a new consciousness: increasing inequality, monopolistic control of production sources, ever-growing student debt, and a worsening climate crisis as a result of the development of our built environment. However, these trends are common among all workers, which is not to say they are not important, or relevant. Rather, in this book I seek to focus on the unique factors that contribute to the forming of a class in the design disciplines.

And finally, it is also important to note that I often use the words "architecture" and "design" interchangeably, especially after the introduction, but even so, much of this text focuses on the specific, concrete conditions of the discipline of architecture, especially through the unionization effort I was a part of. However, because architecture is a major subset of design, and in fact existed long before "design" emerged as a discrete discipline alongside industrial production, I believe many of the lessons learned in our struggle can and should be brought to other design disciplines, and vice versa. As architectural historian Mary N. Woods predicted in the late 1990s, architecture would continue to follow the same process of professionalization, fragmentation, and degradation as medicine and law. Design, equally subject to the laws of capital, is not far behind.[3] Further, what unites us, specifically our engagement in the "creative process," is a major part of the analytical framework for understanding architecture's failed fostering of an authentic class consciousness, as well as building a new labor-oriented one. I hope that designers from other realms will identify with many of these deeply held characteristics.

It cannot be overstated that the work that got us here was a thoroughly collective effort, and I have to thank my comrades, who, without their first steps and determination, none of this would be possible: our Bargaining Committee, Kolby Forbes, Ann Le, and Je Siqueira; the additional founding members of the Bargaining Unit, Po-Yu Chung, Emma Costello, Stephanie Hamilton, Sara Hazan, Praxiteles Lykos, Irshaad Malloy, Brandon Pietras, Paul Rasmussen, Ayman Rouhani, Armaan Shah, Caleb Sillars, and Lauren Uhls; as well as our organizers with the IAM (International Association of Machinists and Aerospace Workers), David DiMaria and Andrew Daley. Though the views of members of BA Union and the IAM are not directly represented in this book, their pioneering efforts in the formation of our union must be acknowledged. My goal in writing this book is nothing more than to underscore the collective work we have done and join the conversation of the labor movement at large by bringing our unique perspective, and perhaps more importantly, learning from the many who have struggled before us.

Introduction

SOCRATES: Suppose, then, Callicles, that you and I were about to take up the public business of the city, and we called on each other to carry out building projects—the major works of construction: walls, or shops, or temples—would we have to examine and check ourselves closely, first, to see if we are or are not experts in the building craft, and whom we've learned it from? Would we have to, or wouldn't we?

CALLICLES: Yes, we would.

—PLATO, *GORGIAS*

The tide of labor is once again rising in the United States. While unionization rates are still low, with only 10 percent of the workforce represented, the shift in the tone of the conversation has been dramatic.[1] Following reinvigorated organizing, many unions have achieved some of the most dramatic wins in decades.[2] As a new generation of workers has entered unprecedented conditions, beginning with the financial crisis of 2008, and continuing with ballooning student loan debt, the end of the neoliberal consensus,[3] a generational pandemic, a continuing reckoning with race and inequality, and an ever worsening climate catastrophe, many have had enough of the status quo. Realizing that they cannot address all of these issues as individuals, workers, particularly from new industries, have turned toward the old political project of unionizing their workplaces, seeking to collectively confront the problems they encounter every day with the hope of translating these efforts to society at large. Tired of the current political means of addressing such crises, many workers now understand that to develop *effective* solutions, they must begin from the bottom, starting with their own material realities, building coalitions that *actually* represent them. Facing the same issues and looking for change in the post-pandemic milieu, my colleagues and I joined the effort and created the first private-sector architecture union in nearly a century.[4]

While groundbreaking, a central question still remains: What took so long? Although almost half of all union members in the United States are professionals,[5] the majority have been historically represented by other occupations, such as teachers, nurses, and technicians, while a small percentage of this "class" are in design and creative industries. With this in mind, it is possible to sharpen the first question: What are the specific barriers that have kept this group not only from unionizing but forming the necessary *class consciousness* to do so? And more broadly, kept it from understanding itself and identifying with labor rather than elitist interests? If possible, what are the implications of such a realignment? However, before such questions can be addressed, which is the central aim of this book, it is important to first look back and examine the broader conditions that have played a role in determining the contemporary landscape.

Historical Origins

Frustration within the discipline of architecture is not a new phenomenon. Writing in the 1970s, socialist architect Harris Stone, self-described as "unsuccessful," echoed the call of the New Left to dismantle the conservative foundations of the discipline, observing that "architecture as it was being taught and practiced served the needs of only the rich and powerful. It had to be redefined. Architecture must become an art which belongs to the people, not to the giant corporations."[6] In the fifty years since, little has changed, the profession still primarily fills the same role of instrument for the ruling class. Working around the same time as Harris, neo-Marxist historian Manfredo Tafuri drew sweeping connections between the agriculture-ideological origins of the United States and the eventual rise and fall of the architect in capitalistic modernism, going so far as to say it is a profession that became steeped in an "atmosphere of anxiety."[7] He concluded his aberrant text *Architecture and Utopia* with a similar call: "Today, indeed, the principal task of ideological criticism is to do away with impotent and ineffectual myths, which so often serve as illusions that permit the survival of anachronistic 'hopes in design.'"[8] Though more pessimistic, Tafuri's critique laid the groundwork for a dormant movement, the beginnings of which we see today.

The reality is, however, that architects and designers have had little to no interaction with the kind of class consciousness found within traditional labor movements. Though the United States has a rich history of labor struggle, which has been suppressed in mainstream histories, there have been few such struggles in design professions. Only in the past decade have issues of labor been front and center in design discourse. For example, recent writing on the topic of architecture and labor has had much success in helping those involved understand what they do as "work," rather than "passion," and the movement would not be where it is today without it.[9] However, the assumption that architects practice a form of art or "immaterial labor" confines the conversation to one about creativity and work alone. While there is comfort in holding onto the artistic origins of architecture and other design-based disciplines, the external forces in which they operate have become too potent to privilege such a reading in terms of analysis, and they have transformed them equally profoundly. In this sense, we might be at a point of no return in terms of the subsumption of design under capital. Therefore, if we are to address the questions above, it is crucial to follow the footsteps of other industries if we want to understand the historical origins through the lens of class.

Though the Industrial Revolution serves as a catalyst for the kind of labor we are interested in, "free" wage labor, that in which labor power is sold in the marketplace in the context of the working day, our story begins much earlier. This contrasts with other design professions. Though the word *design* has origins within the Renaissance in terms of the act of planning a painting, for example, the *designer* as both a product of and actor within history can identify its beginnings squarely within the industrialization of the capitalist economy.[10]

While we will treat architecture as a profession that falls under the larger umbrella of design for most of this investigation, what is happening today cannot be understood without tracing the unique circumstances out of which architectural practice arose, and its drift toward *de facto* design can tell us as much about architecture as it can about labor in the twenty-first century.

Architecture as we know it today, the production of drawings by an individual or team that serve the *central*, authoritative role of both coordinating the parties involved in the making of a future building, as well as the instructions for supervision of constructing it, is a historical development that far predates the development of contemporary working conditions. In other words, architects have been under both a slower form of transformation related to their form of practice relative to building, as well as a more recent pressure from the proliferation of externally developed systems such as technology and finance. And while many of the historical conditions are being undermined or entirely erased in the context of twenty-first century capitalism, they are fundamental in understanding the current state of the profession.

Arrchitectural production can be divided roughly into two main epochs, ancient and modern, which revolve around the role of the architect in the construction process. For many historians, the Renaissance saw a major schism in the development of modern architectural practice:

Prior to the Renaissance, architectural drawings were rare, certainly in the sense that is familiar to us. In the Middle Ages, architects did not conceive of a whole building and the very notion of scale was unknown. Gothic architecture, the most "theoretical" of all medieval building practices, was fundamentally a constructive practice, operating through well-established traditions and geometric rules that could be applied directly on site.[11]

While the architect similarly played a central role in the form of the "master builder," coordinating various individuals on-site, the *building* distinction is key. Integrated into the material construction of the building on-site, the architect was conceived of less as a "designer" and more as the lead "laborer," helping to literally shape materials, solving active construction problems, and generally guiding all the craftsmen not through abstract authority or predetermination, but from the perspective of direct construction knowledge.[12]

The conceptual split between design and construction begins in the Renaissance with the rediscovery of an earlier text, Vitruvius's now famous *De architectura*. Though written centuries earlier, a copy of the manuscript was found in the library of St. Gallen in Switzerland, allowing Leon Battista Alberti access to the ideas that would pave the way for modern architectural design processes.[13] While Vitruvius advocates for a knowledge that is "the child of practice and theory," a balance which in his mind leads to the most authoritative position, Renaissance architects like Alberti became increasingly fixated on the latter, following Vitruvius's definition of theory as "the ability to demonstrate and explain the productions of dexterity on the principles of proportion."[14] With a growing interest in conceptual thinking, mathematical and geometric ideations, and codified principles, along with the parallel development of more humanist pursuits like perspectival painting methods, this schism became further entrenched, widening both the intellectual and physical distance between the architect and the building site.[15]

This estrangement is not only technical but also ontological, for as Marx observed much later: "What individuals are depends on the material conditions of their production."[16] Beyond the substantial transformation in the production of the building, the production of the architect's self-conception was undergoing an equally substantial change: a physical distance from the site of construction, which also meant a newfound isolation. Rather than participating in the collective effort of building construction, one which is *still* collective today, the architect was free to set up a new place of work, one that engendered the development of intellectual exploration and abstract conceptions. Conversely, the construction industry is notoriously slow to change, a rare trade that has been able to resist capitalist forces not limited to labor degradation, automation, and outsourcing. Much of this can be tied to the fact that a building, by its nature, must be built in the very location where it will stand.[17] For the architect, however, this shift from an involvement in the production of the building to the production of ideas—manifested through drawings—placed them in a new social position, one that could more easily identify with artisans and painters, especially in terms of the scale of what they were producing. Though its content is a building, the making of an architectural drawing, at least historically, is more similar to a painting than a physical building.

It is no coincidence that in this same era we see the arrival of one of Leonardo da Vinci's most famous drawings, the *Vitruvian Man*. While Vitruvius's ideas, discovered in the same century, would have been a part of contemporary discourse, we can see more than simply the popular ideas of an era manifesting in a drawing. Perhaps more important, we also see the relation of these principles to the heroic individual. Not only does the work rely on the intellectual imagination of a genius like Leonardo interpreting the difficult abstractions of geometric relationships and their role in the design process, but it also centralizes the *individual* man in this process. This embodiment of the perfected individual expounding abstract idealization of mathematical principles would play a large part in shaping not only the study of architecture, but the self-conceptualization of the architects themselves.

Modern Movements

Benjamin Henry Latrobe, arriving in the United States in 1796 and appointing himself its first architect, articulated the tension between the Renaissance idealizations and the encroaching modern machinations:

> The profession of Architecture has been hitherto in the hands of two sets of Men. The first of those [gentlemen] who from traveling or from books have acquired some knowledge of the theory of Art, know nothing of its practice, the second of those [mechanics] who know nothing but the practice, and whose early life being spent in labor, and in the habits of a laborious life, have had no opportunity to acquire the theory.[18]

This tension observed by Latrobe then firmly establishes architecture within the United States as a direct inheritor of Vitruvius's original dialectic between "theory and practice." Latrobe was also an early manifestation of what sociologist Richard Sennett refers to as the "Americanization" of immigrants who come to America, often leaving behind the more communal settings of Europe for a land with, at the time, seemingly endless opportunity.

Typifying the "self-reliant individual," figures like Latrobe (almost exclusively white men) arrived in a country and shed the broader identifications with ethnicity or religion, for example, and encountered, from their perspective, the fertile soil of a young country primed for a discipline that had long harbored the egos of individual expression.[19] All of these factors set the boundary conditions for what historian Mary N. Woods aptly names the transition of the practice of architecture, and hence her writing on its history, "from craft to profession."

Woods meticulously traces the historical development of architecture as a discipline within the United States, from its humble origin of immigrant European-educated architects like Englishman Benjamin Latrobe and Frenchman Pierre L'Enfant, who learned their craft in esteemed institutions like the Ecole des Beaux Arts in France. Pursuing civically minded work in government institutions, these architects maintained a classical training and disposition toward the arts, but they still experienced a kind of culture shock in encountering the vicissitudes of the untamed marketplace of early America. This latter point is particularly important, as the economy was radically different in the "New World," unstable and full of inconsistent funding between the public and private sector and predicated on cycles of boom and bust.[20] While initially maintaining some roots in the domain of the "master builder," encroaching specialization and fragmentation within the building industry increasingly pushed the architect away from trades, both conceptually and physically. It is in this new economy that the market-based profession, now dominant globally, emerged, further shifting the position of the discipline heavily from craft toward profession during the nineteenth century:

> Office training, with its roots in the artisanal world of apprenticeship, became the common bond, uniting star performers with lesser lights, and antebellum architects with Gilded Age Beaux-Arts designers. The acceptance of professionalism in the United States depended on this linkage between the artisanal and architectural worlds through the office. Learning in an office grounded the architect in workplace realities. The office bridged construction site and art studio, building yard and drafting room; it educated the citizen-architect, who joined art with craft and reconciled private gain with public responsibilities.[21]

As Woods emphasizes, this is not to say that the connection between architect and craft was completely severed; rather, the connection was now *mediated* through both the practical conditions of professionalization and its physical setting, the office, a topic we will further explore in parts 1 and 2. Many architects, no longer artisans working with trades on-site, found themselves cloistered in offices, either working alone or in small groups, neither explicitly a laborer nor an owner, but somewhere in between. In other words, the transformation from master builder to professional worker was complete.

Hence, we now have a summary definition of the conditions of contemporary architecture useful for a broader analysis: typically concerned with a single building, and unable to affect much of what determines the decisions behind what gets built thanks to an unstable and fragmented marketplace and building industry, with one foot in the idealism of theory but more profoundly affected by the entanglements of practice. In this, it is not much different than any other design-based discipline; it is a product of the historical forces leading to the very moment a design becomes reality. As such, we are able to trace an origin to our problem, like most, in the burgeoning Industrial Revolution during the nineteenth-century.

Economist Karl Polanyi's towering work *The Great Transformation* is vital in establishing the implications of this context through what he calls a "double movement," specifically, the development of a market economy that splits political and economic life, at the same time removing interests of social life from certain groups. Identifying three primary groups, the "landed, the middle, and the working class," Polanyi underscores the catalyst to the conditions we find ourselves in today. While the middle classes, where we might for now place architects and artisans, were content to follow the expansion of the "nascent market economy," reaping its rewards, they were ignorant of the degradation being sowed deep below the surface:

> The trading classes had no organ to sense the dangers involved in the exploitation of the physical strength of the worker, the destruction of family life, the devastation of neighborhoods, the denudation of forests, the pollution of rivers, *the deterioration of craft standards*, the disruption of folkways, *and the general degradation of existence including housing and arts*, as well as the innumerable forms of private and public life that do not affect profits. The middle classes fulfilled their function by developing an all but sacramental belief in the universal beneficence of

profits, although this disqualified them as the keepers of other interests as vital to a good life as the furtherance of production.[22]

Without delving further into macro-scale economic trends, an analysis beyond the scope of this book, the implication for design professions is stark: beginning in the eighteenth century, their coerced abandonment of the guild system and integration into the market via small businesses, which leverage wage-labor, came with the unintentional consequence of a proliferating interest in economic service at the expense of their core identity: creative practice. Whether through the forced use of "deteriorating craft standards," or a more explicit pursuit of profit, there is a simultaneous upward trajectory of the business fixation of design with a neglect of making and craft, an observation Woods's historical writing confirms.

Further included in these radical transformations is increased specialization between various trades in addition to ever-expanding technology, which year after year usurps key elements of design craft for its own use. As Marx famously noted during this same time, "Man no longer made use of machines, but machines made use of him."[23] He was talking about the factory system, but this observation couldn't be more fitting for those of us who spend most of our waking lives in front of screens, fixed or portable, a condition nearly universal in twenty-first-century United States.

Returning to Polanyi's analysis, we see that the factor most adjacent to architectural design undergoes a similarly radical ideation: land. Consider Jeremy Bentham, who emphasized the individual's privileged place in Enlightenment ideals, eschewing common property in favor of freedom and liberty.[24] Here, the consciousness of the age is beginning to ossify, the ideals of an ostensibly noble movement seeping surreptitiously into economic and political realms with real material consequences for workers. This reification has a physical manifestation in Bentham's notorious design of the Panopticon, the ultimate symbol of not only state control as scrutinized by Foucault, but in our case, more importantly a symbol of extreme individualization.[25] Instead of a collective of individuals working a shared resource toward common production, the "landed aristocracy," to use Polanyi's categorization, is prized for its self-reliance and ownership of the productive abilities of nature, none of which are possible without the *bought* collective output of the worker. This ethos is materialized in the discipline of architecture and many other forms of design through the rise of the studio system, which utilized a combination of industrialized business organization through the drafting room with individualized tutelage through the master-apprentice relationship.[26]

Today's Problems

While Polanyi's writing is invaluable for understanding the post–Second World War economy, we are now living in a very different set of conditions, felt most acutely in the forms of economic financialization and digital production not present during Polanyi's time. However, the contemporary political implications of Polanyi's work are well understood by political philosopher Nancy Fraser, who reframed his work through not a double, but a "triple" movement. Building on both Marx and Polanyi, the "two Karls," Fraser underscores an important concept from Polanyi, that of the "fictitious commodity," which leads to destabilization through the making of things that should not be commodities into marketized objects, like land.[27] Polanyi would understand design today as a "fictitious commodity," as it is brought into the self-regulating market through professional services in the form of wage-labor, a cheapening of its cost creating a downward spiral in which design is no longer valued and hardly looked at as necessary. This market realization runs directly counter to the common experience for any individual who can appreciate the role design and architecture have played in history through lending its imagination to the beautiful spaces we enjoy visiting—from historic rural towns to large urban centers—much more than the suburban sprawl found in many parts of contemporary America, for example.

Additionally, Fraser sharply identifies the murky distinction between labor and capital today, with a clearer divide "between the thinning ranks of the stably employed, on the one hand, and the swelling precariat on the other."[28] This bifurcation has a profound effect on the smaller sub-sector of design professions; if union density were more solidified, it would be much more feasible not only to raise their own consciousness, but to form unions themselves. Importantly, even during the peak period of unionization and labor-consciousness beginning in the United States in the 1930s, unions in architecture firms were essentially nonexistent. Further, architecture and design, in many senses, literally exist outside of the sphere of production; in fact, they by definition precede production, as does the definition of design itself. For Fraser, the solution is not through "productive" labor alone, but through the addition of emancipatory struggle, which we will address later. However, without denying the overwhelming power of financial capital in today's world or overstating architecture's role in combating it through labor struggle alone, such struggle still could have a unique part to play. Because of the separation from the sphere of physical production, "knowledge" sectors are uniquely positioned to be "needed" by capital, especially in larger cities like Chicago or New York, which mandate strict involvement via building codes and zoning ordinances. This book is an attempt to argue that it not only can be done, but it must be done.

We can return for a moment to E. P. Thompson, as much of his research focused on the artisans and craftspeople, the precursors of the modern architectural and design wage-laborer. In the grievances of the "journeyman Cotton Spinner," we find an eerily familiar description of working conditions, particularly "the loss ... of independence for the worker, his reduction to total dependence on the master's instruments of production."[29] Contemporary designers, through the history we have traced so far, could say much the same. Content to more or less float under the radar and make their clients happy while joyfully toiling away (or "usefully working" as William Morris would say) in their own studios as the glut of suburban housing and other postwar projects fueled the growth of architecture practices and created a reliable path of upward mobility, dissatisfaction was kept at bay. But with the continued strength of the "self-regulating market" and creeping financialization, today's designers identify more with the Cotton Spinner than the self-actualizing pre-industrial craftsperson.

Further, decades of neoliberal policies that have infiltrated every aspect of the economy have not only made the construction, or rather financing, of buildings much more expensive, but the material reality of architectural workers as well. The experience of an emerging architect means an economic condition much more likely to be considered precarious than in generations past. Thanks to crippling student loan debt, notoriously long hours, and a real lack of agency, a new generation of architects is beginning to come to terms with its reality, one that can be described as exploitative. This is on top of the general malaise associated with younger generations finding their way through late capitalism, a series of impenetrable walls and rigged systems benefiting those who have had ample time to concentrate wealth for their own purposes.

We can rely on Thompson to not only diagnose the problem but also to offer a solution. A major part of his historical work is the collection of literature from artisans, which was circulating at the same time as the major shifts in economic production that affected them so deeply: "The Radical and free-thinking artisan was at his most earnest in his belief in the active duties of citizenship.... Since he had been forced to find his intellectual way, he took little on trust: his mind did not move within the established ruts of a formal education. Many of his ideas challenged authority, and authority had tried to suppress them."[30]

Though it is debatable whether we can call contemporary architects or other designers artisans, we can definitively draw a connection between the two, given that they suffered an erosion of craft. During the nineteenth century, this occurred through the gradual replacement of independent, manual methods of making with large-scale and increasingly complex machinery. Today, however, the material craft of all design disciplines has almost been entirely replaced by digital methods of production. Writing about the general degradation of work and skill up until the 1970s, many of the observations Harry Braverman made in his seminal work *Labor and Monopoly Capital* have become sadly relevant for design disciplines today. For Braverman, craft was an essential component of his analysis, as it "provided a daily link between science and work, since the craftsman was constantly called upon to use rudimentary scientific knowledge, mathematics, drawing etc. in his practice."[31] In this way, craft was not just essential to knowledge, but it was also a part of the consciousness of workers and how they understood themselves. This is especially true of architects, as the historic foundation of their knowledge, even today, is built upon the making of *material* models and drawings.

Unfortunately, this is not the case in the professional setting, where the computer is not only usurping traditional methods of manual making, but actually reversing the entire process of production itself. Through software such as BIM (Building Information Modeling) owned by monopolies like Autodesk, computers now make the drawings themselves, while much of the regulatory work of zoning and code compliance is left to the architect—a trend toward de-skilling also threatened by other forms of contemporary automation.

What both of these historical movements have in common is an erasure of scale of making, or a removal of the immediacy of production in favor of larger and more efficient (more profitable) modes of production that further alienate the maker from the process. A connection we might draw is that we still have the intellectual freedom and ability to critically examine the alienating conditions in which we find ourselves and challenge those forces that strongly, yet misguidedly, shape our current understanding of class. As such, the twenty-first-century designer is prime for a radical movement.

Our Work

The historical development of architecture as a discipline solidified its own values which were manifested in very tangible ways in the United States, demonstrating its own dual movement. On the one hand, there was an idealistic pull toward a "gentleman's" profession with participants willing to study under "masters" for little or no compensation.[32] On the other hand, there was a fiercely individualistic practice with equally obstinate professional organizations that were "determined to distance [themselves] from the building trade unions."[33] Here we see the historic roots of architecture's pursuit of idealistic artistic and scientific standards through the exclusive domain of creative genius not only pull it toward an isolating individuality, but also push it away from potent collectivity. Filtered through the workings of late capitalism, with the inherent squeeze of tight profit margins, labor-eroding technology, and individualistic hustle culture, historic ideologies take on an unprecedented anxious form. Though the arc is long, this ideology is at the heart of the practice of contemporary architecture; from the academic studio to the small practice, to the large corporate firm, this dual nature is the overwhelming paradigm of today's discipline.

With this historical context, we could now begin to frame our original questions surrounding class consciousness, and how our unionization effort both fostered this nascent movement and foretold the work that is still ahead.

Though we were a few in a small firm not well known outside of New York City, employees at Bernheimer Architecture found ourselves in circumstances similar to those of many of our colleagues, and more important, our *awareness* of such circumstances was moving from our own individual positions to that of our office and the industry as a whole. And though we lagged behind others, our understanding of architecture's labor problem mimicked that of labor's most traditional industries, which were already deeply affected by capital: "At least in part, dissatisfaction centered not so much on capitalism's ability to provide work as on the work it provides, not on the collapse of its productive process but on the appalling effect of those processes at their most 'successful.'"[34] Prior to the twenty-first century, architecture would have certainly been deemed a "most successful" product of capitalism, the demystifying of which is at the center of our investigation. All of us were trained in a discipline that promised upward mobility and job placement through technical higher education, complex skills development, and creative problem solving. This book will explore many of the deep issues that have only been touched upon so far, but first a brief overview of our process is helpful for understanding the deeper context behind this burgeoning labor movement.

The initial unionization effort did not begin with Bernheimer Architecture, but a more well-known firm, SHoP architects. This unprecedented campaign set its sights high, targeting the firm responsible for Barclays Center and several other prominent skyscrapers throughout New York City, many now half-occupied, the result of unfulfilled investments for international billionaires. An initial vote was promising, but after extensive intimidation, union busting, and other bizarre behaviors from the partners, the organizing committee was forced to pull its petition.[35] Though unsuccessful, Architectural Workers United (AWU), an organizing campaign out of the International Association of Machinists and Aerospace Workers (IAM), continued its work in seeking more appropriate partners for labor. The events at SHoP were common knowledge, sparking a fervor in architectural offices in New York City. Sitting with the aftermath, workers at BA found themselves in new territory. While we had started informal organizing efforts in 2019, beginning substantive conversations about how we would like to see our workplace change, this work was derailed with the onset of the COVID-19 pandemic. Though disruption was acute not just to our organizing, but to life for everyone around the world, a new tool emerged out of the chaos of the early months of the pandemic: online meeting. As we, like many other professional workplaces that were fortunate enough to be able to do so, developed a new form of digital working, one that facilitated more private conversations, we also hired a former SHoP employee, bringing their experience from the narrowly defeated unionization effort. With the combination of someone with knowledge of unions (and contacts at the IAM), and meetings that were easier to hold than ever, the groundwork was set to form the first private-sector architecture union in at least a century.

Some initial interest began with a few members of the office, with the blunt but somewhat startling question leading the way: "Do you want to unionize?" It didn't take long for an early, yet small, consensus to emerge. While we were on foreign terrain, we were more than ready for the challenge. Years of conversations about the viability of the profession, including low wages, increasingly astronomical student debt, severe lack of representation, burnout, and stagnation in addressing broader issues of affordability in housing and climate change in the building industry, all contributed to the perfect conditions for the formation of our union. Generally feeling alienated from most decisions impacting our general well-being and standing, ours was not just a fight for fair pay, but also a fight for dignity and respect, a common theme in unionization efforts.[36]

An organizing committee took shape, and we began having conversations that we had never had before. Rather than merely venting or exposing frustrations, we asked everyone not only what their most important issues were within the office but those in the industry at large. We wanted to hear both what wasn't working, and more important, what practices might look like if things *were* working. Time and again, we heard about problems in our office, not in isolation but in conjunction with how those problems stemmed from industry-wide deficiencies. Some six months later, after many rounds of productive conversations, question answering, and education for both us and our employer, we announced that our principal, the owner of the firm, had voluntarily recognized us, creating history not only through the formation of the union but also in the collaborative nature of the process. In negotiating our first collective bargaining agreement we utilized a new hybrid form of negotiation that emphasizes a collaborative over an antagonistic approach.[37] This decision, both the voluntary recognition and the format for negotiations, has set the tone for our process, made possible by the best aspects of a medium-size architectural practice:

informality, a connection with everyone, and a general desire for goodwill among all parties. While there have been significant disagreements between management and employees, as is the case in any workplace, we have sought to demonstrate to other campaigns that an antagonistic relationship between the two is not necessary for the formation of a union. We know that many other architecture offices *do* have such caustic relationships, but we believe that a contract that is collectively bargained is something that all workers deserve, and an integral part of forming solidarity between architecture, design, and other forms of labor.

To begin the process, our office wrote a collective statement to reflect our shared goals in shaping our internal values and those of the industry at large. We viewed this as an important step since we were the first to embark on this labor journey. Here is our statement:

> The staff and management of Bernheimer Architecture are proud to announce that the employees of Bernheimer have organized the first private sector union of architectural professionals in the United States under a voluntary recognition agreement, becoming some of the newest members of the IAMAW through their AWU (Architectural Workers United) campaign.
>
> We recognize that both the employer and employees in the field of Architectural work face constraints and challenges beyond the control of any individual firm, and that by working together we can uplift the profession and industry in ways that we could not by acting alone. Reflecting on these challenges and opportunities, we will embark on this collective work centered on the following values:
>
> - **RESPECT:** We believe that all of the work we do begins with treating each other with unconditional respect. If we want to create safe, beautiful spaces that truly benefit the communities they are designed for, we must first recognize the unique value that each team member brings to our work.
> - **VALUE:** If we respect our team, we will also fully value their

labor. This means equitable compensation for all, regardless of race, gender, or position.
- **GROWTH:** We also recognize that a healthy profession begins with a healthy education. The work we do in creating an effective office structure and work environment is directly connected to how we educate future workers.
- **TRANSPARENCY:** We seek clarity in how decisions are made internally and externally, ranging from individual employee career development to complex project funding sources.
- **IMPACT:** The complexity of the problems facing architecture and the built environment are enormous, from the pervasive influence of capital to devastating climate change. Though we, as one practice, cannot impact these forces alone, we believe that forming and recognizing this union is a crucial step toward building solidarity industry-wide and will have a meaningful impact.

Architecture is a creative and wide-ranging discipline, bringing together many of the sectors and challenges we face today. Within this discipline, BA has been a progressive office at the forefront of design, craft, and quality, affordable housing.

Though we are stepping into uncharted territory in many ways, we are overwhelmingly excited, and hopeful, to bolster the values that make BA special. We encourage and invite other practices to join us in this endeavor to reshape the industry at large.[38]

With our values shaped, we could formally begin negotiating, not on exclusively adversarial grounds but instead strive toward something in common, ideas that could hold each side accountable throughout the process. To that end, hybrid negotiations allow for input from both sides of the table in the form of issue identification and brainstorming, with the result that proposals are created through democratic conversation. Traditional negotiating has advantages, especially on economic issues like wages and 401(k) contributions. While we utilized it for certain portions of the contract, the IBB/hybrid process creates an open table situation where workers do not feel subordinate to management, but equal. Requiring unanimous consent, workers have the ability to effectively veto proposals they might feel unfairly benefit management, and while the same is true of management, it gives workers the ability to speak open-mindedly, an opportunity less afforded in other forms of negotiating. Through this collaborative process we have been able to negotiate over traditional economic issues, but maybe more important, we as the union have had real input through a democratic exchange, allowing us to co-design how the office itself works. Some of the key highlights of this process include:

1. Just cause: real job protections for workers, a first in the industry.
2. Definition of roles and responsibilities for employees through a new staff organization in lieu of ambiguous roles.
3. Creation of a Labor-Management Committee, which allows for collaborative decision-making regarding issues outside of the contract.
4. Professional Development and Mentorship programs with a focus on employee-driven growth.
5. Technology provisions that require the input of staff and necessitate the dignity of human-centered labor, a key issue related to the emergence of Artificial Intelligence.
6. Complete flexibility in hybrid and remote work policies that privilege employee working arrangement needs.
7. A 36-hour workweek with the ability to compress from five to four days, allowing employees to attend to the needs of everyday life outside of the office, humanizing how and where we work.

These are just a few of the elements of our historic union-made contract, providing a new type of safety net to architectural workers, the first of its kind in the industry.[39] The above protections and conditions are unheard of in most architecture offices, and while limited for now, they provide a tangible standard that other offices can point to should they initiate unionization. Because we are the first private-sector architectural office to utilize collective bargaining, this contract is both about our own workplace and a possible precedent for others. Only a sample, this new agreement is not just about improved job conditions but bringing dignity and value to the designing of work itself. Too many workers are locked out of the decision-making processes that impact their day-to-day lives, even though they naturally have some of the best ideas toward addressing them. As the late labor organizer Jane McAlevey wrote: "Power for ordinary people can be built only by ordinary people standing up for themselves, with their own resources, in campaigns where they turn the prevailing dogma of individualism on its head."[40] If founded on this spirit, unionization is one of the most effective tools toward combating the entrenched individualism that has plagued design since our introduction to the Vitruvian Man.

Economic wins might be slim in practices on thin margins, as is true of many architectural practices, but collective bargaining, especially in this form, brings real democracy to the workplace, a fundamental means for tackling the more existential issues that all workers are experiencing in late capitalism.

This leads us to the exciting yet fraught moment in which we find ourselves. While the significance of this first labor win should not be minimized, it is still just that, a beginning. In order to foster this nascent movement and expand its goals beyond exclusive protectionism, it is necessary to explore the roots of the discipline's stubborn resistance to change. In what follows, beginning with Part 1 of this book, we will move from the detailed process described above to a more historical and philosophical investigation into the *creative consciousness*, the sum total of the forces that have been internalized in designers. Though other industries might be concerned with more tangible issues, those like architecture and design are too mingled with concepts like creativity, which are notoriously difficult to articulate, and these become even more so when considered together with issues of class. Therefore, a large portion of this work attempts to unpack and expand these deep-seated questions. Such a consciousness, predicated on the creative, in reality occasionally appears as a false consciousness, specifically compelling creative professionals to align with a conception of themselves as a "privileged status group," and this discourages them from identifying with the interests of an "exploited class." The results of this creative consciousness are also explored, underpinning the ways in which design and creativity are exploited in the workplace, as well as how a credentialism buttressed by such self-perceptions creates a privileged yet ultimately impoverished profession.

Part 2 of this book is situated in our current conditions, demonstrating how design professions might begin to raise a new kind of *class consciousness*, not through the complete abandonment of creativity, but on the contrary, supplementing it with an understanding of designers as workers. This new class consciousness will require emulating other forms of labor that have already adopted it, such as the construction industry and other professions, as well as articulating architecture and design's unique position between labor and capital. Once adopted, a new theoretical and practical conception of liberation *through* design becomes possible, reaching beyond the exclusive confines that design has found itself in and beginning an orientation toward the most pressing problems of the broader society.

Part 3, more of a beginning than a reflective investigation like the parts that precede it, begins a conversation with three specific issues: gender, race, and ecology. Though there are many more issues equally worthy of attention, these are three areas in which design has had a complicated, and disappointing, relationship, and three to which I believe design could best lend its own insights. Further, this section is distinct in that it is less systematic, forgoing a linear analysis and instead treating its content in a collective, integrated comparison, reflecting how the very call for a liberatory design could allow it to lend its problem-solving skills toward these areas, but also shape its own identity and values.

Now, we begin the work Tafuri called us to do, reaching the inception of a movement that carries the *potential* for dramatic change:

> Only at this point—that is, after having done away with any

disciplinary ideology—is it permissible to take up the subject of the new roles of the technician, of the organizer of building activity, and of the planner, within the compass of the new forms of capitalist development. And thus also to consider the possible tangencies or inevitable contradictions between such a type of technical-intellectual work and *the material conditions of the class struggle.*[41]

It is crucially within the realm of class struggle that we hope to bring our newfound "ideology," as well as our material action. With a theoretical framework developed through critical theory and labor not only architecture, but also those design disciplines that have ossified further since Tafuri's time, might be better prepared to bring unique forms of thinking and creativity to the crises of our own time. Designers now must seriously, in the words of Peggy Deamer, "rid themselves of their antipathy for labor discourse."[42] Rather than identifying with the class that is paying them and which has determined too much of their material conditions, designers might shed their outdated aspirations and instead begin to identify with the workers who make their designs a reality, a first step into forming a new class consciousness. With this, a new possibility emerges, the beginning of a new "cross-class" form of solidarity with traditional laborers and other social movements. Design has ignored labor for too long, but we are in a moment in history where continuing to do so is not just a missed opportunity, but detrimental to the future of both.

PART 1

Creative Consciousness

> The distinction between profession and craft is at first difficult to make, yet it is of great importance. The craftsman survives so long as the standards for judging his work are shared by different classes. The professional appears when it is necessary for the craftsman to leave his class and "emigrate" to the ruling class, whose standards of judgment are different.
>
> —JOHN BERGER, *ABOUT LOOKING*

Phases of Design

The transition away from creativity (and its integration with real craft) within design disciplines has been long and complex, and it is difficult to pinpoint specific moments of profound change.[1] In some ways, the transition is not entirely complete, as many of the vestiges of craft remain in the daily practice of design offices and strongly shape the identities of those who operate within them. As such, the task of unwinding the tangle of craft, work, professionalization, and class is a difficult one. A place to begin is a procedural overview of the process of design, from start to finish. Because of the complexity of designing a building, a process that encompasses many of the pressures, techniques, and situations that all designers face, examining this process through the perspective of architecture and its workers provides as much context as possible for application to other spheres.

Architectural practices generally operate in a strict procedure of phases. Beginning with any pre-design meetings and preparations, projects shift into three core design phases and one for construction, in the following order: Schematic Design (SD), Design Development (DD), Construction Documentation (CD), and Construction Administration (CA).[2] Each phase grows in complexity in kind and amount, shifting from considerations of spatial organization, siting, environmental factors, usage, program, and other "large" questions to increased technicality, specificity, and detailed documentation for implementation. This is not unlike the process of development for other creative acts, especially those that must manifest in physical things, as it is more natural to begin in abstraction and end in concrete application. However, the space allotted for craft shrinks as the phases progress, with more attention demanded by code, consultant requirements, and other forms of technical compliance. Though this has always been the case as the issues in the realm of technicality must eventually be answered, those in the realm of craft have also progressively diminished in every phase, especially since the introduction of the computer into this process. The totality of this development provides a large part of the answer to the question of why professionalization has taken such a strong hold over design disciplines.

For our purposes, we will consider the perspective of the architectural worker through these phases. While the numbers vary based on the size of a given project, the typical team in an architecture studio will consist of either a Principal (firm owner) and/or Project Manager with a team of Designers, or workers, below them. Beginning in SD, the tasks of the Designer are to help analyze and establish the site boundaries of the project, identify the needs of the client, and in general help frame the bounds of the project before it begins to take shape. Here the tasks are largely clerical, the

Designer responsible for taking notes while the Principal directly engages with the client, documenting the site through photography and measurements for translation into the computer, and helping to organize any subsequent digital files that are created through this process. Gone is the drafting table and paper ledger, every surface translated long ago onto the computer screen.

As the vision for the design begins to take shape, the Designer is responsible not for the vision itself, since this comes from above, but for the *manifestation* of the vision. This is not to say that there is no creativity or craft involved in this process, since Designers are usually handed half-baked ideas, which must be turned into clear and readable drawings and models. These ideas are often ambiguous, such as an offhand remark to change something, or "napkin sketches," physical scribbles that take little time to make with the hand but substantially more hours to convert into a presentable digital format. A part of this early process that has remained concrete is the selection of finishes and other building materials, common to all designers whose end product is something physical, such as furniture and textiles.[3] During this early phase, if they are lucky, the Designer might even be granted permission to design a small portion of the project itself. However, it is *always* a hierarchical process, as the Principal has ultimate control of what the design will eventually look like. This ambiguous back and forth are the first inklings of the conflict between manager and worker, a struggle that shapes the issues central to this chapter.

Once the design has been schematically shaped, it must be clearly articulated in a set of drawings for review and approval by the client. This set, the capstone of the SD phase, is the first major deadline of the project, bringing about the pressures associated with a definitive timeline for completion. Zoning and code analysis, site and floor plans, elevations and sections are all encompassed in a holistic document that captures the scope of the design. This also includes the clandestine bits of text and legalistic compliance structures that must be present in the set but are largely unread, not unlike user agreements for software. With the content provided by the Principal and Project Manager, the Designer will spend hours compiling these various documents while simultaneously fielding revisions to the design. This process of revision, known as "redlines," typically extends up until the deadline, with surprise requests from the client or second-guessing from the Principal or Project Manager lasting until the last possible moment. Juggling completion and revision is a large part of the work of the designer, creating a sense of instability throughout the process.

The next phase (DD) sees the vision become more concrete, transitioning from an idea to something more buildable. In this, typically stressful phase, the Designer is responsible for the previous phase's tasks, but in a more intense condition as new and more detailed forms of compliance must be folded in. In essence, while the steps are largely the same, each is more involved, with more information progressively layered into each drawing. Here the use of multiple forms of software is critical, the necessary files existing in both real and unreal space. As the drawing set grows, so too grows the number of pages in the drawing set that must be maintained. Depending on the scale of the project, the Designer might either be responsible for the entirety of the clerical management of the drawing set or given dedicated portions. Regardless, the hierarchy of the previous phase is still present, the Designer facing power-based pressures from above and technical pressures from below. During this phase, craft-based acts have been most strongly erased over time. With the computer gaining control of what was at the hand of the Designer, consultants have also become a critical part of this phase, their expertise in the proliferating systems of a twenty-first-century building requiring differentiated knowledge. The Designer might not be required to know how electricity is generated from solar panels and transmitted to both a battery and individual apartments, for example, but they are required to ensure that this information is present in the drawing set.

The final design phase (CD) is more or less a carryover of the previous phase with the primary intention to create documents that can be successfully used for construction. All craft is relegated to the design of details for construction, with the holistic shape of the project already formed. Even in this last phase of creativity, much has been ceded to technology and consultants, the Designer acting as more of a conduit between ready-made digital components and their use in the software in front of them. Receiving pre-packaged files for proprietary wall assemblies, for example, the Designer must coordinate with the product representative in order to receive the files in the correct format. Once obtained and made useable, the components are then integrated into the existing drawings, a process akin to the assembly of a car or other complex machinery. This is only one instance of an endless list of such convoluted informational integration processes. Thoroughly embedded in the drudgery of producing hundreds of technical and bureaucratic drawings, the Designer is at this point months (possibly years) beyond those first exciting moments of the project. With relative autonomy and flexibility long out of view, craft is all but abandoned in order to comply with the ever-present demands of project delivery. At the end of this phase, the Designer, through the visionary direction of the Principal, and the day-to-day management of the Project Manager, has contributed countless hours to a complied drawing set that is ready to use as directions for the construction process. Though they might be involved in the work of Construction Administration (CA), the primary tasks of the Designer are complete, an object ready to manifest from the many lines occupying the many (digital) sheets of the drawing set.

Throughout all of these phases, the milieu of the design office is one composed of slick monographs, old material samples organized in bins, a wood shop that is gathering several layers of dust, and the products of that shop, meticulously made models proudly displayed on shelves, rich material explorations of the past with little hope of new ones joining them. While the designer is affixed to their contemporary tool box, the computer, the ghosts of material creativity haunt their every click.

To an outside observer, this design-based process might appear extraordinarily different from other forms of professionalized or "white-collar" labor. And in many ways, the observation would be correct: though craft and creativity have faced enormous pressure both in the development of these phases and external forces, they are still very present in architecture and design disciplines, for it is inarguable that the process of imagining something from nothing, with an intimate involvement in the entirety of this process, is a unique and deeply creative pursuit. While other disciplines might also technically "make things appear," such as accountants and their once blank spreadsheet, the consistent connection with imagination and the new realities that shape our material world set the Designer apart. Numbers, equations, and finances also shape our world, but they remain abstractions in a way that designed objects do not.

However, in the context of the *historical* development of design, this kind of work has changed dramatically, its form creeping ever closer to typical professional and administrative services. What has specifically changed is the amount of time the Designer spends working through such creative areas, with more and more time dedicated to compliance rather than design. In other words, many parts of the design process have become thoroughly professionalized. However, since creative acts are the catalyst for any design process, even if the time spent doing them is decreasing, they maintain an elevated cultural importance.

The question is whether this elevated importance is helpful or harmful for the identity and struggles of the twenty-first-century Designer. The idea of the "creative genius" has been thoroughly challenged, yet it remains stubbornly embedded within design disciplines. In this way, it is not enough to focus criticism on idealized concepts, but rather to trace the origins of its development and its ongoing impact. With the process-based context of the design phases sketched, we can now begin to unmask those embedded forces that are both deeply human and abstract, beginning with creativity. Doing so is critical in order to understand not just how, but *why* identification with creativity remains in tension with the counterforces actually shaping design today.

Creativity and Design

Creativity is one of the core elements in any design process. Here it can be conceived as a particular quality that links disciplines or expressions such as art, music, and design. Popularly, it is treated as a personality trait that distinguishes certain individuals from others. Alternatively, some draw a firm connection between creativity and craft, considering it a humanist attribute that connects any activity undertaken by people, for example, from the carpenter to the lab technician.[4] Though various disciplines share many attributes through the common denominator of creativity, for our purposes we are primarily concerned with those aspects of creativity that inform design, and vice versa. However, an important difference between creativity and design is that design has a more concrete identity, while creativity is ephemeral and difficult to define. If we keep this difference in mind, we can begin by rebuilding a definition of design that produces a broader conceptualization of creativity, which can then allow for the consideration of social implications.

The etymological root of the word *design* is the Latin *designare*, which literally means to "mark out." Sharing origins with the fine arts, works like paintings were "designed" with representational underlays before the final application of paint was applied. In its simplest sense, to design is to articulate the extent of something, ahead of time, whether a sculpture, product, or a building. This typically takes the form of a drawing, the lines on paper marking out an objective or true representation of the intended design, often forgoing the use of perspective so that scale may be used to translate dimensions from the smaller drawing to the full-size construction. Physical models might also be used to investigate more complex 3-dimensional spatial conditions, beginning with a smaller, simpler version of the final idea. There is certainly an element of problem-solving coded in all definitions of design, an important qualification that differentiates it from art, but for the purposes of understanding its connection to creativity, a more stripped-down definition is appropriate.[5] It is also important to conceptually maintain some links to art for this analysis, as many of the ideological struggles of design workers are muddied with this self-understanding predicated on creativity. With more widespread adoption in the early 1500s, the term *design* generally began to imply the separation between an initial plan and its eventual realization, which became architecture's modern origins. Though during this period *design* and *making* were more directly intertwined, today there is a sharp boundary between the two; very few designers are actually building whatever it is they are conceiving.

This emphasis on the planning performed ahead of externalized labor is, surprisingly, lauded by Karl Marx in chapter 7 of *Capital*, Volume 1:

> A spider conducts operations that resemble those of a weaver, and a bee puts to shame many an architect in the construction of her cells. But what distinguishes the worst architect from the best of bees is this, that the architect raises his structure in imagination before he erects it in reality.[6]

The key differentiation, according to Marx, between man and animal is the ability to project forward, an occurrence before the act of creation itself. It is this ability to conceive of potentialities, that is, ideas, assemblies, schematics—designs—that allows for the production of complex structures and objects. Marx is not afraid to celebrate this distinctly human ability, noting that when people are in active engagement with materials provided by nature "he realizes [*verwirklicht*] his own purpose in those materials."[7]

In other words, our direct engagement with the material world is a primary way in which we create purpose and meaning in the world. Contemporary writers such as Glenn Adamson, a curator and historian, are sharply aware of this purpose Marx speaks of, articulating it as "material intelligence," even extending the notion beyond traditional design disciplines:

> Material intelligence plays a notable role in science, too. It is easy

enough to caricature artisans as instinctive, and lab technicians as analytical. In fact, craft-makers possess extraordinary reserves of technical knowledge, while experimental scientists often talk about the importance of having "good hands." The same goes for medicine. Caring for the human body demands much more than a knowledge of anatomy and chemistry—it's a tactile business. Doctors and nurses routinely use touch to rapidly and accurately develop diagnosis. And as for surgeons, show me one without material intelligence, and I'll say: thanks, but I'll have my operation elsewhere.[8]

Adamson is correct to emphasize the importance of "material intelligence" in contemporary practice. Important to Marx, who was operating in a more material world due to the lack of such advanced technology, was the necessary cooperation of collective labor in order to physically manifest these preconceived ideas into actual, material realities. Yet, from the perspective of capital that initiated the production of commodities through design, the individual is emphasized, ideas attributed to a single origin of conception. In actuality, a collective effort is necessary to manifest the design, which is arguably embedded with more design thinking than the initial conception itself. Though cooperation is a key component of Marx's critique in *Capital*, even he succumbs to the notorious mystification of individualization of design, praising the singular architect's achievement in creating complex objects, for we should remember that architects are not responsible for actually making buildings themselves, but the instructions required for building them.[9]

Contrary, and yet complementary, to this understanding of design is the fixation on objects common in the discipline. Whereas Marx's modest definition of design reinforces individualization, his emphasis on concrete, material forces is in direct opposition to the historically dominant reliance of the *hylomorphic* model of thinking in the design process. Anthropologist Tim Ingold posits that, beginning with Aristotle, the way in which the Western world thinks about *things* relies heavily on conceiving them as *objects* with *form*:

To create any thing, Aristotle reasoned, you have to bring together form (*morphe*) and matter (*hyle*). In the subsequent history of Western thought, this hylomorphic model of creation became ever more deeply embedded. But it also became increasingly unbalanced. Form came to be seen as imposed by an agent with a particular design in mind, while matter, thus rendered passive and inert, became that which was imposed upon.[10]

As we have noted, designed objects are not any less susceptible to capital's voracious desire to commodify everything, and the hylomorphic model plays a special role in reinforcing this condition by doubly objectifying those things that are both utilitarian (that is, solve existing problems, the ostensible goal of design) but also exhibit a unique design quality. A quintessential example of this is the iPhone, a brilliant object from a functional viewpoint, intuitively combining the utilities of the phone, internet, email, etc., but which quickly evolved into a status symbol. Today, Apple can be viewed less as a design firm and more as a brand. This is only one example of how in contemporary society design operates as what Henri Lefebvre would call a "mask," shielding individuals from the concerns of their real lives.[11] A product that is only concerned with meeting such "masked" needs would look very different than the iPhone, and Apple's slick marketing and spectacle-based product launches would be deemed unnecessary. Instead, the product becomes an expression of identity, the association with the brand a projection of status.

Interestingly, the concept of creativity itself is being reexamined and questioned, with writers like Samuel Weil Franklin observing that the idea of creativity arose in very particular conditions in the United States during the Cold War. With the perceived threat of communism rising across the globe, creativity became a useful mechanism for American advertising agencies and industrial designers as a way to distinguish their work from the hyper-rationality and conformity of the Soviet Union. Further, Franklin stresses that the concept of creativity did not exist prior to capitalism itself, instead emerging well into the 1900s as a means to address the tension between increasing productivity and consumer culture:

> The concept of creativity, typically defined as a kind of trait or process vaguely associated with artists and geniuses but theoretically possessed by anyone and applicable to any field, emerged as a psychological cure for these structural and political contradictions of the postwar order. Psychologists developed tests to identify "creative people" based largely on the need of military and corporate R&D, but they were also motivated by a larger desire to save individuals from the psychic oppression of modernity. Likewise, in industry, the first creative thinking methods, such as brainstorming, were initially geared toward industrial improvement and new product development, but they did so by addressing alienation on the job. Advertising professionals touted "creative advertising" as both a cure for lagging sales and a way to bring individual vision back into their field. And many corporations embraced creativity not only to help spur innovation but also because it made them look more humane amid backlash against the military-industrial complex. In all of these cases, the practical matters of staffing R&D labs, coming up with new product ideas, or selling said products coexisted with larger concerns about conformity, alienation, and the morality of work.[12]

This certainly still aligns with industries we would consider "creative" today. And though it has suspect origins, we are, for better or worse, stuck with the term as it seems to speak to something true about a way to distinguish certain kinds of work. However, while offering a diagnosis, Franklin's work does not help to fully unearth the nature of a discipline that emerged well before modernism, an origin that might serve as a means to reorient creativity and design away from commodification and toward something more useful.

Returning to our ancient Greek thinkers, civilization at this time did not categorize these kinds of occupations and ways of being based on how they *thought* or a *quality* they possessed, to put it in terms understandable today, but what they *did*. In other words, confirming Franklin's hypothesis, the personal quality of *creativity* would not be used, let alone the adjective *creative*, and instead the noun "*tekhnē*" would indicate the *thing* that someone made through a particular *practice*. Socrates, in several of Plato's Dialogues, specifically measures craftsmen on the objects of their focus, and the actions that lead directly to the making of those objects. In the *Gorgias*, the question as to what constitutes a true tekhnē, or craft, is at the heart of the dialogue, with Socrates spending many of his words defining, and more important protecting, real, useful craft from the Sophists who sold a fraudulent tekhnē in the form of rhetoric:

> SOCRATES: Well now, let's see what we're really saying about oratory. For, mind you, even I myself can't get clear yet about what I'm saying. When the city holds a meeting to appoint doctors or shipbuilders or some other variety of craftsmen, that's surely not the time when the orator will give advice, is it? *For obviously it's the most accomplished craftsman who should be appointed in each case.* Nor will the orator be the one to give advice at a meeting that concerns the building of walls or the equipping of harbors or dockyards, *but the master builders will be the ones.*[13]

Rather than labeling these makers as culturally "special" or "unique" like the modern subjects of Franklin's analysis, Socrates continually frames the beginning of arguments through an explicit, specific example of tekhnē that has a directly measurable output: the painter and the canvas, the doctor and bodily health, the engineer and city walls. In this way, he is cleverly subverting the famous Sophistic doctrine from Protagoras that "man is the measure of all things"; for Socrates, real *productiveness* is the measure of all things.

We live in a very different time than that of Ancient Greece. Today's Sophists no longer claim that man, but *capital* is the measure of all things. Our reality in the throes of late capitalism is much more aligned with the subject of Franklin's writing. But since our work is not just critical but also aspirational, we shouldn't be too quick to throw out the outdated yet wise words of the Greeks. We might then be able to, for the moment, isolate Plato's understanding of tekhnē, as one that is *socially productive*, still conceptually connected in some way to the modernist notion of creativity as it is associated with the realization of imagined things, but distinct from it in that it is not concerned with profit or irrationality. In other words, Plato's definition of craft is ultimately concerned with social well-being both from an individualistic and collective perspective.

Similarly, the contemporary attempts via Franklin to understand "creativity" are incomplete, still missing a broader structural analysis, placing too much weight on the superficial emergence of the concept, and no remedy other than an idealistic reframing of the idea of creativity. While this might be too much to expect from a work of history, for our purposes it is important to move beyond this limited approach, one that relies on conceptual abstraction rather than a broad, systematic reorientation based on concrete conditions. Helpful in many ways, we still remain in a state that treats creativity as a status-based adjective, a notion with force that still engenders false consciousness.[14] While Plato might offer us some ancient hints, there is further work necessary to uncover the origins of a creativity specific to architecture and design.

Origins of the Myth

In order to understand how design perpetuates itself through its own unique form of fictitious commodification,[15] reinforcing the "cult of creativity," it is important to first examine the origins of its mystification, a development that occurred in the time between Socrates and Franklin. While the historical forces we have examined so far certainly shape the practice and identity of contemporary design, a critical examination of the manifestation of such developments can reveal the barriers impeding significant change today.

Though common to all professions, the academy plays an oversized role in the shaping of not only designers' skills, but more important for our examination, their identities. The design studio, grown out of the craft guild system, is a collaborative form of learning that sharply differs from more industrialized, and individualized, forms of education. However, this does not make it any less prone to the forces of capital it will eventually confront in professional practice; it merely makes this confrontation unique. In this educational sphere, design studios not only help designers develop their particular skill sets, but also serve as the proving ground for the exploitative notions that eventually metastasize into powerful forces. However, a difficult contradiction is that although the myths are born there, the academic studio-based environment is one of the last places of unadulterated creative pursuit, existing in a premarketized state. As such, the line between simultaneously existing creative agency and creative exploitation is difficult to discern. In this section, the typical architectural design studio can serve as a vehicle for the examination of specific principles that speak to the eventual barriers that arise in the professional/economic sphere.

The educational paradigm of design disciplines, and creative disciplines in general, is in direct opposition to the industrialized learning model, or what educator and philosopher Paulo Freire would refer to as the *banking* model. Non-design disciplines typically rely on a model of education that utilizes the direct deposition of knowledge from an authority figure. On the other hand, design-learning exhibits something closer to Freire's insurgent *dialogical* learning model, with students becoming critical co-investigators in continual dialogue with their instructors through group critiques, open-learning studios, and non-deterministic problem solving and making.[16] At its best, this model draws its strength from precluding one-party learning; rather, both student and teacher learn and teach simultaneously and interchangeably, a profound subversion of typical power structures.

The architectural studio environment is a quintessential model for how design disciplines utilize dialogical pedagogy.[17] In this classic studio-based education, the teacher coauthors an architectural project with the student rather than dictating operative design approaches. Courses begin with the introduction of deliverables (square footage, use, site, etc.) but subsequently develop through posing problems, not simply solving them. Although there are aspects of architectural education that require direct dissemination, the majority of learning in studio courses consists of students discovering their own design processes and projecting their own visions.[18] Much of this endeavor asks students to articulate individual problems, manifested as qualitative questions: *What is the environmental context of this site? What creative principles will I develop to organize the assemblage of materials around the programmatic constraints? Who will ultimately use this space, and how will they use it?* Through many conversations with their instructor and classmates, students collectively refine, reject, and sharpen their ideas, creating a feedback loop that is less measurable by specific benchmarks and more on the assimilation of the parts.

Here we can observe one of our first distinctions from other learning models, that while the problems are initially given to them in some form, there are an infinite number of possibilities for each student to confront. The antithesis to this would be a mathematics course in which the struggle proceeds *until* a singular correct answer is discovered. Established formulas are literally followed, creating a linear approach to answering problems with narrow solutions. Though the mathematics student might satisfy a part of the definition of creativity regarding the "production" of something new, in their case a novel answer to a given problem, the means of arriving at this solution is through the fixed medium of numbers and the machines that generate them. Conversely, in the architecture studio, paths diverge with the widest possible array of answers and means of getting there. Further, a solitary solution delivered discreetly on a sheet of paper to the teacher is not enough; architecture students must share their ideas with both their instructors, and most distinctly, with their peers, through drawings, images, models, written research, diagrams, and all available means of dissemination. Equally important here is the process of iteration, which involves reproducing many versions of the same concept in order to begin to answer questions that do not have straightforward answers. Again, other disciplines might also repeat problems or experiments as a form of iteration, but what distinguishes design is the unique combination of the open-ended nature of the resolution and the distinctly dialogical (social) means of arriving there. The studio space itself reflects the special social situation, each student's desk holding individual material explorations directly adjacent to their peers, papers and models spilling in between.

Not only is the development of the student's work dialogical, but so too is the process of review, or critique, common to all art and design educations. Typical university courses for other majors involve prescribed exchanges in which the finished work, such as a paper or an exam, is delivered to the teacher, who then proceeds to grade the work based on a predetermined rubric. Alternatively, the studio critique is a fluid experience, which, through rich discussion, ends with many uncertain conclusions. Though guest critics may arrive with their own agendas and use the critique to espouse their own philosophies, the conversation nonetheless revolves around the ideas and work that the *student* produced. In this way, the student's work serves as a filter through which to test ideas, not only their own, but also those of the outside critics. This reciprocal process of intense criticism is a strength among all designers, the hours of dialogically reviewing their own work and that of their peers creating a sharp and discerning eye. Most important, the ideas put forward by students during critiques are those that define the nature of the dialogue, underscoring their authorship, participation, and ultimately, their agency.

Based on these principles, we can draw a distinction between dialogical, authentic forms of creative acts and those that are professional—that is, filtered. As a result of this kind of rich, nuanced learning, students, acting through *real* creative agency, will work late into the night, continually testing and revising ideas due to the ambiguity of what constitutes an "answer." They push their visions as far as possible, knowing this will enrich the feedback during the often ambiguous critique. Not only do conceptual issues increase the intensity of labor, but also the material reality of design-based education: making drawings, models, and other objects takes a substantial amount of time relative to other academic work.[19] Viewed holistically, engagement with design-based education provides students with an autonomous act of creative pursuit. This, coupled with a rich material-based education, is an increasingly rare reality that should be commended and broadened, and one which is useful for future propositions.

The intellectual intensity developed during this critical time of learning emerges with a concurrent reality, that of a *mystification of the design process*, a process that is fully revealed upon entering the professional arena. Regardless of the worker and discipline, a certain "universal" process begins upon their integration into this office-based realm, one of homogenization, efficiency, and productivity: "In this sense, the modern office becomes a machine which at best functions well only within its routine limits, and functions badly when it is called upon to meet special requirements."[20] The ruthless efficiency of the machine-like office observed by Braverman *immediately* catalyzes the degradation of the design worker; though masked in excitement at the opportunity of producing "real" work in the "real" world, they are, at least subconsciously, aware of the acute differences between the studio and the office. Braverman underscores not only the operations of the office, but also the effects of such intensity on the workers themselves:

> On the contrary, not only does their skill fall in an absolute sense (in that they lose craft and traditional abilities without gaining new abilities adequate to compensate the loss), but it falls even more in a relative sense. The more science is incorporated into the labor process, the less the worker understands of the process; the more sophisticated an intellectual product the machine becomes, the less control and comprehension of the machine the worker has. In other words, the more the worker needs to know in order to remain a human being at work, the less does he or she know. This is the chasm which the notion of "average skill" conceals.[21]

Here, workers are not only wrapped up in the machinations of a new environment, but they also simultaneously find the skills and craft they spent years developing being either eroded or completely abandoned, a trend that if true in the 1970s when Braverman articulated it, is even more potent today.

However, the designer confronts not only the "modern office machine" like other professionals, but also a transfiguration of the unique ethics that had been intimately developed during their educations, hardly recognizable in their new environment. This manifests in several ways, chief among them being three key ethics: 1) the design process is never finished, 2) the more labor time involved, the better the results, and 3) design is an individualist, cerebral act accessible to a privileged few. The last of these ethics, though a compelling topic in terms of understanding design's broader relation to its adjacent industries, and falsely developed in opposition to the collective nature of the studio, is less relevant to the current analysis. As such, the first two ethics are more relevant in terms of deconstructing the internal contradictions that constitute the nature of design. Through the above examination of a design education, the origin of these ethics is apparent. What is less clear is the consequences of these ethics in the transition from an academic environment to a professional one.

Within the process of mystification of the design process, the designer continually returns to an increasingly unfamiliar condition, one in which the dual characteristics of 1) creative pursuit and 2) compulsory force (the new ethics) commingle in the form of a body of muddled values. Encountering this new "field of design," designers enter their first true state of *alienation*, noted by Braverman in the degradation of craft, while still maintaining a connection to the original state of real creative agency. Subjected to each new compulsory ethic, the former becomes foggier, and the latter slowly usurps it as the new dominant paradigm. This cyclical process lays the groundwork for a smooth transition out of the educational sphere to a total assimilation of the designer into a professional setting, an environment in which the new ethics overwhelmingly dominate any notions of unbridled creative pursuit. In other words, subjected to new values, the designer is conditioned for a particularly intensified form of exploitation.

While the first two ethics manifest most particularly during education, the third, that of "individual genius," does not become fully palpable until the designer is embedded in professional practice, as we will see later. Engaging in hours of discrete creative discovery, again, admirable during education, also creates the conditions for a strange struggle: individuals who simultaneously have a deep sense of creative autonomy but are also willing to bequeath that very agency to a higher authority ordained with a more specialized "creative capital." Here, an underlying struggle is also present, as the previous ideological associations with art become most apparent. As we have observed, for much of history, design, and especially architecture, have had a close association with the fine arts, with design programs of all stripes either intellectually or physically placing their university programs within close proximity to fine arts programs. At the very least, it is typical for design students to begin with foundational courses before entering their official studio sequences, taking drawing classes that are indistinguishable from the classes that their arts-based peers might take. This is a logical formation of education for design has been conceived as a fundamental part of art for hundreds of years. So embedded is this understanding of design, a potent form of ideology, that even the fiercest critics of architectural practice today are dependent on this narrative for their criticism, elevating these components of the discipline as its highest aspirations.[22]

Considered in sum, the ethic of individual creativity fostered historically and through education becomes subverted to further the aims of the individual owner of the practice. What is consistent with all the ethics, however, is their thorough indoctrination during education, which becomes nearly invisible when transmuted to professional practice. If ever candidly discussed, these ethics are viewed less as guiding principles and more as unquestionable dogmas, truths that carry the field forward. Those monographs that adorn the shelves of the studio (for designers prefer not to refer to their workplace as an office) are the physical manifestations of these ethics, celebrating uniquely talented practices whose namesakes follow the vision of the individual principals who own them. No longer a form of practice in the sense of an action, design becomes a quasi-ideology, imposing its will unknowingly on anyone who becomes embedded in its special sphere of labor.

The professional sphere, the arena which young designers find themselves abruptly thrown into after they emerge from the academic studio environment, relies on a thoroughly inverted version of the shared principles. Though many practices are quick to outwardly embrace the actual forms of creativity of the studio environment, inwardly they appear more like any other business, obeying the ethics of capital instead of creativity. Here too we can begin to examine the critical intersection of not just creativity and design, but a third essential component, class.

Creative Consciousness

So far, much of our analysis has been limited to the *internal* qualities of creativity and design: in how they came to be, how they are uniquely intertwined, and how these forces shape a distinct kind of worker. The sum of these forces can be understood as a holistic definition of creativity within design. Equally important, though, is the articulation of a public understanding of what these elements are, both from mythologized and effectual perspectives, which we can consider *external*. Although both are certainly real in the sense that they affect the real, everyday lives of people, we have been able to demonstrate that those qualities that are internal seem to possess a more authentic nature as they have emerged in situations with fully human, creative activities. It is where the internal and external meet, however, that design's most stubborn impediment to full class-based realization is created, that of *creative consciousness*.

Today, contrary to historical definitions and origins, the word *design* is essentially synonymous with *luxury*; for a designed object or space to enter public discourse, it must be exceptional. And to be exceptional, it must be expensive. The implications of this necessity manifest in the designers, too. Fashion brands, for example, utilize the name of elite individuals to market their unique appeal. If we are to examine the broader social implications of this misconception, sociologist Max Weber can offer some clarification on the ambiguous term "status," an important concept related to the self-identification of certain groups. This concept can also help us to understand the genesis of current economic and labor misalignments (or negative attitudes toward them) among design professionals. While Marx sought to define class exclusively on economic grounds, Weber sees another component that influences both actions and conceptions of individuals in society:

> In contrast to classes, *status groups* are normally communities. They are, however, often of an amorphous kind. In contrast to the purely economically determined "class situation" we wish to designate as "status situation" every typical component of the life fate of men that is determined by a specific, positive or negative, social estimation of honor.[23]

Articulating this new category, Weber then identifies the manifestations of it: "In content, status honor is normally expressed by the fact that above all else a specific *style of life* can be expected from all those who wish to belong to the circle."[24] As we move through society, we see evidence of this "style of life" everywhere in regard to designers: the predominance of black above all other colors, off-beat eyeglasses that are sure to stand out, a keen eye for innovative and "undiscovered" brands, an eschewing of the vernacular and/or other mainstream forms of culture, and overall a refined and distinguished sense of identity. In sum, the desire to stand out in a particular way, which signals to others that we are different, and that we belong to a small, exclusive cohort. Put another way, "With some over-simplification, one might thus say that 'classes' are stratified according to their relations to the production and acquisition of goods; whereas 'status groups' are stratified according to the principles of their *consumption* of goods as represented by special 'styles of life.'"[25] In other words, class is only about the relationship of individuals to the making of goods, while status, a more expressive category, and thus one of predominance for Weber, is about *consuming and displaying* such goods. One only need visit the MoMA store to see the commodity-based expression of this within design.

We will return later to the need for a reorientation back to a holistic framework of class, which emphasizes exploitation. But while the goal might be to make such "superficial" demonstrations much less substantial contributors to the development of class consciousness, we cannot simply ignore that status is an *actually lived part of everyday life*.[26] In fact, it is easy to reduce the Weberian concept of status to exteriorized forms of commerce—for example, clothing or the films or television shows someone watches. However, there are also professionalized realities that confuse the sharp distinction between production and consumption. Additionally, the self-admitted "over-simplification" of Weber glosses over another interstitial economic component, that of access to such stratified status groups through exclusionary gatekeeping. The evidence of the effects of this "reified" self-conception is in the tendency not just for designers but professionals at large to use an exclusive form of credentialism to distinguish themselves from others and protect their own work from other pernicious economic factors.

Sociologist Frank Parkin goes so far as to equate credentialism in terms of importance in the conversation of class with that of property rights, a central tenet for Marx of course.[27] Building on Weber's analysis, Parkin emphasizes that there has been "the attempt by an ever-increasing number of white-collar occupations to attain that status of professions. Professionalization itself may be understood as a strategy designed, among other things, to limit and control the supply of entrants to an occupation in order to safeguard or enhance its market value."[28] Designers are not immune to this proliferation of professionals, though their self-identification with art and craft might strongly resist it. While architects underwent the process on the eve of the twentieth century,[29] today we see many more disciplines added to the ranks as a result of Franklin's conditions, as well as ever-increasing specialization. Graphic, UX, web, fashion, interior, landscape, furniture, and industrial designers, to name a few, all have their own forms of specialized credentials and associations, which are only growing.

Further, Parkin effectively underscores why this form of credentialism should be considered interstitial, or at least distinct from traditional forms of economic struggle via trade unionism. Though there has been some history of labor unions organizing skilled workers in order to limit their numbers, their primary contribution has been in organized opposition to those who own the means of production so that they might win economic concessions. Professional closure, on the other hand, is an entirely different strategy:

> Credentialism, on the other hand, cannot be seen as a response to exploitation by powerful employers; the learned or free professions were never directly subordinate to an employing class during the period when they were affecting social enclosure. Their conflict, concealed beneath the rhetoric of professional ethics, was, if anything, with the lay public. It was the struggle to establish a monopoly of certain forms of knowledge and practice and to win legal protection from lay interference. The aim was to ensure that the professional-client relationship was one in which the organized few confronted the disorganized many.[30]

Two elements in this passage provide key insights to the cognitive workings of design professionals today. First, credentialism was not, and still is not, about addressing *exploitation*, especially in the Marxian sense; it can only create a status-based protection while excluding others from participating. If one is concerned with an emancipatory or broadly participatory society, there should be obvious problems with this. Second, the closure is primarily concerned with a "monopoly of certain forms of knowledge," a fundamental linkage between what is both conscious and unconscious in workers. Thus, we can begin to draw the connection between the broader implications of status-protected knowledge and the form of its design professionals lay claim to, that of "creative" knowledge.

First, however, it is important to return to the idea of creativity as an isolated concept in order to answer the following question: If we now understand how "status consciousness" plays an active role in the constitution of design professionals, how is creative consciousness determining the relations, even if falsely, or misguidedly, between these same individuals?

Though writing primarily on class *consciousness*, Georg Lukács defines the *unconscious* component of class formation as a concealed yet potent force to be reckoned with:

> Regarded abstractly and formally, then, class consciousness implies a class-conditioned unconsciousness of one's own sociohistorical and economic condition. This condition is given as a definite structural relation, a definite formal nexus which appears to govern the whole of life. The "falseness," the illusion implicit in this situation, is in no sense arbitrary; it is simply the intellectual reflex of the objective economic structure.[31]

The task, then, is to uncover the "definite formal nexus which appears to govern" the life of design professionals at large. It is important to underscore that for Lukács, reading Marx, class "is determined by position within the process of production,"[32] meaning it is exclusively a question of economic relations. Though the origins of "creativity" are indeed ancient, it is also important to emphasize those productive qualities in the footsteps of Socrates, for a "creative" actor, whether a practical designer or aspirational artist, must earn a living through one form of wage-labor or another.

To summarize, this unconscious aspect of "creativity" is a simultaneously *passive and active force*. On the one hand, it is expressed through *positive* movement toward both authentic expressions of artistry *and* petty-bourgeois values such as individualized expressions and exclusive styles. On the other, it is an equally powerful *negative* identification with issues of economics, labor, exploitation, and ultimately political struggle.[33] In order to challenge creative consciousness and its "false unconsciousness," then, its origins must be uncovered and potentialities enlightened.

Through this analysis, we might enrich, and question, the implications of the traditional economic thesis by interrogating a less explicitly connected type of false consciousness specific to creative consciousness. By virtue of the ambiguity in relation to the traditional litmus test of production, it is a problem worth confronting as methods of work continue to shift away from traditional industrial production. This investigation might also liberate "creativity" from the confines of petty-bourgeois ideology, as Lukács suggests, and instead reorient itself toward productive, emancipatory labor.

Creativity, understood in this "presented" form, reveals itself in society "externally," more in line with Marx's concept of the "commodity-structure," a "'phantom-objectivity,' an autonomy that seems so strictly rational and all-embracing as to conceal every trace of its fundamental nature: the relation between people."[34] We can now continue to demystify the societal, status-based consensus definition of creativity as something special or exclusive, more akin to a "law of nature," or individual merit, by critically thinking about how workers in design industries relate to their specific means and methods of production rather than their specialized credentials or accolades:

> The more closely we scrutinise this situation and the better we are able to close our minds to the *bourgeois legends of the creativity of the exponents of the capitalist age*, the more obvious it becomes that we are witnessing in all behaviour of this sort the structural analogue to the behaviour of the worker *vis-à-vis* the machine he serves and observes, and whose functions he controls while he contemplates it. The "creative" element can be seen to depend at best on whether these laws are applied in a relatively independent way or in a wholly subservient one. That is to say, it depends on the degree to which the contemplative stance is repudiated. The

distinction between a worker faced with a particular machine, the entrepreneur faced with a given type of mechanical development, the technologist faced with the state of science and the profitability of its application to technology, is purely quantitative; it does not directly entail *any qualitative difference in the structure of consciousness.*[35]

Here Lukács identifies the real consciousness is the relation of the worker to how they specifically make their work, an argument that supports the universal ownership of creativity among all workers, not just artistic.

This alternative conception of creativity allows for a new understanding of design workers, not with special inherent qualities or a misleading sense of status, but by the *material* tools and processes that they actually interact with. Such a reframing underscores the dual reality that design workers are indeed different from other workers because of their own unique relation to a particular productive process, but similar to other workers because of their equivalent economic relations, that is, class. By decoupling the notion of creativity from the specific methods of work, then, we can lay the groundwork for raising consciousness on two fronts: 1) through not abandoning but still fostering the ways in which design professionals do not exclusively *own* the concept of creativity, but utilize specific forms of creative making, or *tekhnē*, in their own work, and 2) relating this work to broader societal movements through its reframing as labor by leveraging their privileged position among all workers not for exclusive personal gain, but for the support of broader emancipation.

As discussed, the contemporary societal consensus is that to be creative is to be special; from the Apple ad that launched the corporate design behemoth we know today[36] to the "cult of creativity" that bestows special status to individual artists and designers, those who leverage their unique visions and effective problem solving, in addition to appropriate sums of capital, are rewarded with an extraordinary privileged status. Yet, it is important to qualify this position; mistakenly labeled as the "creative class" by mainstream sociologists,[37] there is nevertheless a *false* condition, in the Lukácsian sense, which presents itself as *true* reality in the form of status:

> Status-consciousness—a real historical factor—masks class consciousness; in fact it prevents it from emerging at all. A like phenomenon can be observed under capitalism in the case of all "privileged" groups whose class situation lacks any immediate economic base. The ability of such a class to adapt itself to the real economic development can be measured by the extent to which it succeeds in "capitalising" itself, i.e. transforming its privileges into economic and capitalist forms of control (as was the case with the great landowners).[38]

Expanding on Weber's notion of status, Lukács aptly describes the position designers occupy in twenty-first-century capitalism: amassed cultural clout in the form of certain privileges, but besides the "superstars," a tenuous economic position in regard to the relationship to production. It is this latter relation that especially helps us understand a crucial component for pivoting toward a stronger class consciousness: exploitation.

Design as Exploitation

In our current economic paradigm, creativity appears more widely in its mythological form rather than its productive form. This apparent, status-based understanding of creativity is real in the sense that it affects the daily lives of those who live under it. However, it is also an integral part of the "false consciousness" described by Lukács. Although we have articulated the development of such a false-consciousness, specifically through *creative consciousness*, there are also methods worth examining that leverage such positions in order to control and exploit those most prone to its workings. This exploitation further inhibits design professions in the sense that it not only weakens the individual's ability to pursue a truly productive form of *tekhnē*, but it also weakens the collective efforts of entire professions at large, with industries favoring credentialism and gatekeeping rather than inclusion and expansion. However, the roots of such systemic incapabilities begin at the level of individual workplaces.

Passion for unfettered creative pursuit, in conjunction with the ethics previously described, and a uniquely American obsession with "doing what you love" for work, creates the perfect material conditions for exploitation of the students transitioning to the design workforce. But what exactly is it that is being exploited? Returning to *Capital*, Marx's central theory of surplus-value can serve as a useful parallel in articulating the nature of exploitation in design practices.[39] Surplus-value is more clearly understood through the lens of a traditional factory, or through companies that produce physical things, and even service jobs that work on a strict shift schedule. In other words, a measurable amount of profits are directly generated by the work and subsequent products that the individual laborers produce. After the worker regenerates the value necessary for the employer to recoup the cost of production, every extra hour worked becomes profit for the capitalist.

However, this economic situation does not directly translate to professional design offices because they usually operate on extremely thin margins compared to developers and other large clients (a fact often used to justify exploitation),[40] and more importantly, because the nature of what exactly it is that they produce is ambiguous. This "knowledge" economy has thus evaded much of the scrutiny that traditional workplaces have received, but there are more similarities than seem obvious. If it is not *excessive* surplus monetary profits that are produced, then what is? And how does it ultimately get exploited and leveraged?

One hint lies in Marx's definition of surplus-value, specifically that value which manifests as an apparition:

> The worker does indeed expend labour-power, he does work, but his labour is no longer necessary labour, and he creates no value

for himself. He creates surplus-value which, for the capitalist, has all the charms of something created out of nothing.[41]

This ghost-like manifestation of Marx's surplus-labor finds its equivalent in a form of surplus-*creativity* in design practices, its nebulous nature exerting the ethics over design workers.

Acknowledging the creative skills that students develop during their education, a direct linkage can be made from indoctrination through design ethics to their eventual exploitation by the firm. Even before they enter practice, new employees emerge in the market carrying unprecedented levels of student debt. The most backwards part of this condition is that the student of design has been forced to pay tens of thousands of dollars to develop their own creative process, a gross commodification of creativity itself. Now in the workplace, a particular type of economic relationship with the employer supersedes the relation with the teacher, one more akin to indentured servitude over exclusively "free" labor. Argentinian activist and author Veronica Gago, whose work is examined more deeply in Part 3, astutely draws the connection between these forces: "Debt functions by structuring a compulsion to accept any type of work in order to pay one's future obligation. This capture of the obligation to future work initiates the exploitation of creativity at any cost: it does not matter what type of work you do; what matters is paying your debt."[42] In other words, the young designer is immediately placed in a structurally weaker position than a "neutral" wage-laborer, dependent on a paycheck not just for basic necessities, but also as a means to service ever-increasing amounts of debt.[43]

With the economic relationship skewed toward precarity, the traditional forms of exploitation are amplified. As employees, design workers are typically charged with the task, from their managers or their principles, to finish the work, but also to arrive at the *best* design idea. Leaning on the principles developed in university, a low-level worker, or designer, will rely on a particular expression of design ethics, that of iteration. However, *endless iteration* also means *endless toil.* Though any designer will agree that testing multiple versions of a specific idea or concept is a crucial part of achieving a better outcome, the line between necessary and unnecessary iteration becomes barely perceptible, extending the working day toward an ever-distant horizon. Further, the strength of criticism developed in the academic environment simultaneously becomes the worker's greatest weakness. Though the designer might have initial confidence in an idea or scheme, always lurking in the background is the latent potential for a critique from the manager. Trained to embrace criticism as vital to the design process, the design worker is always dutifully ready for revisions to their work. This ambiguity also exerts an especially strong form of control, keeping workers in a state of uncertainty, never certain if what they have done is enough.

In terms of historical class conflict, the shift length, that which defines the length of the working day, was a powerful negotiating tool, as it neatly delineated time between hours of labor and hours of leisure. The nature of design work, on the other hand, and the knowledge associated with it, is ambiguous; it is difficult for a worker to know when to stop the process of creativity during their daily labor, when to draw the line between what is productive and unproductive. While a purported day is from 9 a.m. to 6 p.m., there is no explicit shift change or bell to indicate that the day is over (a common problem among salaried workers). If the request from the boss requires finding the "best-designed" solution, it is impossible to know exactly at what moment this plateau occurs. Though the majority of design bosses do not *explicitly* require working long days, there is a powerful, *implicit* understanding that being a good employee means exhausting all the possibilities of the project. In other words, it means the exhaustion of the workers themselves.

This prolongment is common to other professionals, whether the adjunct professor who must attend more administrative meetings and teach larger class sizes or the nurse who is asked to take on more patients than the year before. However, what distinguishes design from other kinds of work is the ambiguity of the task at hand. Because the act of designing involves imagining something that does not yet exist but must operate in the real world, there is nearly an infinite number of possibilities to answering the given problem. For the medical professional, a general "best of practice" exists to solve the immediate problem at hand—for example, how to treat pneumonia. For good reason we do not seek novel remedies every time a patient arrives at the hospital with such ailments; the established procedures are important for implementing treatment as quickly as possible. However, when asked to design a new piece of furniture or home, the design professional has a blank slate to work from, with the ability to draw on a wide history of inspiration in order to propose novel solutions that best fit the client. In fact, many clients hire designers to directly challenge what has come before and provide a solution yet unseen.

With design workers, perhaps simultaneously willing and unwilling participants in this endless cycle of iteration and exhaustion, firm owners are provided with a highly educated and motivated pool of talent that is willing to pursue the best design at all costs, surplus-creativity extracted until the last drop. Endless iteration not only means endless toil, but the endless production of ideas. Here the owners of the firm are the overwhelming benefactors of the designs generated, the worker's solutions achieving a better product than possible without them. This well-vetted design is then exchanged with the client for both monetary profit and prestige, for the one with the name on the door, the owner, will always receive the most credit.[44] In many cases, the exploited even become so entrenched in the daily machinations of the office that they are unaware of the reinforcing of their own exploitation. As sociologist Erik Olin Wright observes:

> One of the ways of reducing the overhead costs of extracting labor effort is to do things that elicit the active consent of the exploited. These range from the development of internal labor markets which strengthen the identification and loyalty of workers to the firms in which they work to the support for ideological positions which proclaim the practical and moral desirability of capitalist institutions.[45]

"Internal labor markets" in design offices include the awarding of more face-time with clients, design decision-making privileges (not to exceed the Principal), appearances at academic studio reviews, international trips to projects worked on by the office, and other small spheres of superficial authority and agency. Workers caught in this self-reinforcing "internal labor market," are not surprisingly some of the most effective and stalwart opponents to workplace reforms such as unionization, adopting the ideologies that are most beneficial to management, which create a cult-like sense of belonging.[46]

The academic studio environment is deeply intertwined in professional design environments not just ethically and socially, but also economically. Because many design disciplines are made up of a relatively small workforce, firm owners tap former students for employment, initiating a pipeline of always available talent that is willing to enter the continued tutelage of their academic role models, now surreptitiously transformed into bosses. This cyclical form of coercion takes a unique shape among design disciplines: what appears as endless paper pushing in other white-collar jobs manifests instead as dedication to a cause, muddying that work which is important and that which is redundant, ultimately allowing for an acute and prolonged form of exploitation and control. Combine these working conditions with the absurd economics of the student-debt crisis, and the result is an entire generation of indentured servants who are prime for exploitation of the surplus creativity generated for their respective firms. If workers are forced to pay a substantial portion of their paychecks toward an insurmountable debt, there is low probability that they will take such risks as starting their own practices, the very places that could offer them their fullest sense of creative agency. Young workers also know that in tightly knit design industries, word-of-mouth recommendations are essential for future success, further compelling them to not "rock the boat" and uphold the status quo in order to remain employable.

Though services that lead to the creation of objects at all scales, from smartphones to buildings, involve large teams and many hands with varying levels of creative intelligence, it is those who own the firm who receive the external recognition. In the case of one of the most popular designed objects ever made, there is a subtle distinction between those who design objects and those who make objects: for example, the epithet found on the packaging of every iPhone, "Designed by Apple in California," which shrewdly fails to acknowledge who, in reality, makes the physical thing. Through such common paradigms, surplus-creativity not only leads to the creation of the "best" product possible for the benefit of the owner, but also a specific type of capital, that of *design capital*. Similar to "cultural capital" in the vein of Pierre Bourdieu, design capital has less directly observable economic benefits, but more social ones: "It is not the relative value of the work that determines the value of the name, but the institutionalized value of the title that can be used as a means of defending or maintaining the value of the work."[47] Leveraging the surplus-creativity generated by their workforce, firm owners spend this unique form of capital not in order to purchase goods like the traditional capitalists, but instead on ephemeral things like publicity, recognition, coveted teaching positions, and a *cultural* (not necessarily a monetary) petty-bourgeois lifestyle. This type of capital is real in that it creates extra-privileged positions for the few directly built on the backs of the many.

One material example of the effects of exploited design integral to the false consciousness among design workers is the unnecessary division between "manual" labor and "intellectual" labor or, in more academic language, between "productive" and "unproductive" labor. Though there are qualitative and material differences that are vital for consideration of specific policies, such as health care considerations, the differentiation for the purposes of class consciousness values one form of labor over the other. Harry Braverman, who spent his working life in both manual jobs in various welding and metal-working operations, as well as in "intellectual" ones such as editing and writing, saw the distinction as ineffectual:

> Labor which is put to work in the production of goods is not

thereby sharply divided from labor applied to the production of services, since both are forms of production of commodities, and of production on a capitalist basis, the object of which is the production not only of value-in-exchange but of surplus-value for the capitalist. The variety of determinate forms of labor may affect the consciousness, cohesiveness, or economic and political activity of the working class, but they do not affect its existence as a class. *The various forms of labor which produce commodities for the capitalist are all to be counted as productive labor.* The worker who builds an office building and the worker who cleans it every night alike produce value and surplus-value. Because they are productive for the capitalist, the capitalist allows them to work and produce; insofar as such workers alone are productive, society lives at their expense.[48]

This can cut both ways. While the bricklayer might resent architects for their privileged position of instruction (and expression of identity), the architect always carries a certain level of anxiety, knowing deep down they are not physically responsible for making the building. We will return to this point in the next section, but it is worth emphasizing now, especially in the context of Wright's observation that workers can help perpetuate their own exploitation. This kind of bifurcated understanding of labor serves only to divide, weakening both groups. Instead, each should be seen as different, but no less necessary, parts of the process of making a building.

Specialized, Neutralized

Previously we examined the professional environment in the context of the new designer's emergence into it, in other words, a process of transformation. Here we can examine the eventual results of such a process. Accordingly, we need not limit this examination to design itself, but expand it to encompass relations to other disciplines. The combined pressures of mythologized design ethics, exploitation built on surplus-value and surplus-creativity, and the continual incursion of technology into the labor processes not only distance design professions further and further away from the material world, but also drive them closer to the digital and scientific. Though this trend is hardly unique to design disciplines, it is critically important to them because of both their inherent connection to the material world and their ability to solve problems through alliances with other disciplines and movements.

Incorporating Glenn Adamson's material understanding of designers, it is evident that they are at least in some part engaged with the *making of physical things*. However, this engagement with the physical has been degraded through increased mechanization manifested in the office environment. While designers have a special, dualistic (abstract-concrete) knowledge of material reality, it is intertwined with, but distinct from, the historical proletariat's knowledge of making physical things.[49] In this dichotomy, between creative consciousness and its engagement with material making, the position of such knowledge can be diagnosed in the specialization, and hence weakening, of its potential for change.

A contradiction within this progressively immaterial situation is that as individuals become more specialized in their fields, the further they are removed from the immediate processes of the making of the things they design. For the making of even relatively simple objects such as a chair, for example, the litany of consultants, contractors, and technicians involved are not individually specializing in the sort of material practices that might be expected of a master chair maker:

> This [specialization] tends to obscure awareness of the extended production chains through which materials, tools, components and packaging are sourced. Nobody—not an assembly-line worker, not a CEO—has a comprehensive vantage point. It is partly a problem of scale: the wider the view comes, the harder it is to see clearly what's close at hand.[50]

While specialization has been a near universal historic trend, the advent of mechanized production and digital technology (*not* technology in the historical productive sense of *tekhnē*) has shifted the focus of our collective bandwidth from the material to the immaterial, from the general to the specific, from making to managing.

Even the act of establishing a design-oriented office is something that can't be done without the aid of a sub-specialist. Before the computer was a necessity of office life, one could go to the store and buy the tools required for creative work: drafting boards, pencils, brushes, paper, gouache, were all immediately accessible both in terms of time and space. Marx's observation that architects are designing and thus always working with the future draws an interesting distinction between design workers and those workers who make the things that they are designing—a dialectic between ideas and material. Nonetheless, before the advent of the computer, designers could at least relate to other workers in that they themselves produced physical documents, even if they were "immaterial" in the sense that they served as instruction to eventually make physical things (think of a furniture designer making the assembly instructions for a mass-produced chair, for example).

However, during most of the history of creative professions, drawings *were* created manually on paper; the "digital turn," to borrow a phrase from historian and critic Mario Carpo, is a relatively recent phenomenon.[51] Today, one must consult an IT company to aid in the purchasing of not only computers, but also in establishing a server for file sharing and management, unique logins for computers, drivers for printers, etc. When surveyed, the necessary infrastructure for a twenty-first-century office is truly staggering, and much of it is hidden.

Considering this hyper-technological matrix, it is becoming increasingly difficult to call designers by that name. Rather than designers who implement technology, they are becoming technologists that occasionally implement design. The sheer amount of software, plugins, and programs for which they must have working knowledge serve only to further alienate them from the thing that originally brought them meaning: fulfilling creative pursuit. The very workers who ostensibly have the greatest sense of agency are slipping toward Marx's "individuals burdened with this drudgery":

> The lifelong speciality of handling the same tool now becomes the lifelong speciality of serving the same machine. Machinery is misused in order to transform the worker, from his very childhood, into a part of a specialized machine.[52]

Just like the workers in factories before them, designers are succumbing to the overwhelming forces of capital, their identities subsumed by the very machinery, in this case software, that simultaneously distinguishes their skills and specialties. Though a fine line, this trend is an overwhelmingly negative one.

Dominated by the specializing demands of technology and mystified ethics, designers today are embedded in places of work that lack any autonomous principles. Although much of this work is critically important to social concerns (architects working on housing, industrial designers on new medical equipment, graphic designers making public documents), their reality is siloed from other social concerns that are tangentially important to those who complete the work. This fall from social necessity is apparent in the colloquial use of the word *designer* not as a noun but an adjective describing luxury goods such as handbags and cars. A critical reframing of these disciplines through the lens of working-class consciousness presents the only possibility for reorientation toward the pressing concerns of our time.

Due to a lack of criticism, along with a long history of professionalized "othering," the idea of design professions building solidarity with traditional working-class industries has at times been framed as absurd and misguided, from the perspective of both classes. There is a long history of "critique" in many arenas of life, from reason to religion and nearly everything in between, as Henri Lefebvre articulates, but design thus far has managed to evade such a level of scrutiny.[53] While Richard Florida refers to designers as the "creative" class, writer Matthew Stewart might more broadly define it as part of the "9.9 percent" and "the new American Aristocracy."[54] Whether Stewart believes, on the one hand, that design professionals fall into this category and as such should be held accountable for their consolidated socioeconomic clout, or, on the other hand, they fall more neatly into a traditional understanding of the professional middle class and therefore should focus their disdain toward this new aristocracy, many contemporary cultural writers of this kind continue to draw sharp distinctions between the professional and working class, reinforcing traditional binaries.

Design professions should be held accountable for their own self-identification with petty-bourgeois values (a third class ambiguously used by Marx),[55] a result of the potential for independent, craftsman-like autonomy, but also of social forces pushing these disciplines toward spheres with more social power. Though an understandable goal, it should be noted that this alluring creative autonomy is becoming increasingly unrealistic. Even if designers do become independent entities, they will likely fail to resemble the self-sufficient craftsman of the late eighteenth century, as the rapidity of bifurcation within design disciplines due to technological specialization yields increasing interdependence rather than independence.

Nevertheless, like Braverman, sociologist C. Wright Mills argued that even though much separates the professionals and traditional manual laborers, there are many shared realities, including that of alienation:

> Among white-collar people, the malaise is deep-rooted; for the absence of any order of belief has left them morally defenseless as individuals and politically impotent as a group. Newly created in a harsh time of creation, white-collar man has no culture to lean upon except the contents of a mass society that has shaped him and seeks to manipulate him to its alien ends.[56]

Design professionals find themselves in a similar situation, even though they occupy a higher place on the social ladder. In many ways, this seems a natural consequence of jobs shifting from manual labor to office or service labor. Nevertheless, this occupation of a strange middle ground prevents professionals from practicing solidarity with other popularly conceived of working-class industries. This intermediate position is both tenuous and privileged.[57] The technicians/professionals are situated such that they experience multiple/contradictory class positions while finding it difficult to produce agency in this milieu: "The white-collar man is the hero as victim, the small creature who is acted upon but who does not act, who works along unnoticed in somebody's office or store, never talking loud, never talking back, never taking a stand."[58] Though Mills's portrayal is bleak, it depends upon a nuance that could allow for a new type of agency to develop for technicians. This provides a helpful conceptual flexibility, contrary to orthodox Marxists such as Nicos Poulantzas, who relies on a rigid definition of exploitation based on industrialized productiveness.[59] Such positions can become so convoluted that in the effort to understand social classes, Poulantzas must exclude himself from the class of "real workers" because as an academic he does not technically produce anything physical.

There is a particularly strange example that demonstrates the agony wrought by such a rigid conceptual framework. Poulantzas uses the case of a strike at a company in which the contradictory nature of the positions of such employees is laid bare since they might either not strike, and thus be aligned with ownership, or participate in the strike and "temporarily" be aligned with workers, even going so far that each of these activists counts as a switching of class.[60] Though he grants this "temporary" working-class position, even in the case of fervent support in striking, the professional will always permanently be considered bourgeois since it would "undermine the objective definition of classes made by Marxism" to consider them workers. As we have seen in the rise of academic labor organizing, the reality around us is different, with much union attention today focusing on student workers and part-time faculty, an expansive approach that allows for the potential of broader coalitions than traditional organizing targets. But by statically placing such workers in the bourgeoisie class as Poulantzas does, we risk remaining stuck in unhelpful definitions of professionalization and labor dependent on specialization and distinction.

Contrary to such divisive positions, as a larger portion of the labor market is professionalized, it is important to create a class consciousness that is more allied with traditional labor than that of the managerial class. Unfortunately, the latter has had a much larger influence on design professionals than the former. Though some of the founding members of the first professional architectural organizations in the United States, such as Richard Upjohn, aspired toward the "collective action" of building trades, as many emerged from the tradition of the master builder, they sought to distinguish themselves, instead exemplifying architects as gentlemen first.[61] Today's professional associations like the AIA (American Institute of Architects) surely have conformed to this vision, prioritizing legalistic contracts, bourgeois galas, and awards for accomplished firm owners, with little to nothing to say about the burgeoning labor movement within the industry.[62]

If solidarity with traditional working-class groups is to happen, design professionals must remove the "mythologizing mask" that shrouds design and instead become conscious of their unique position relative to the material world. They must intentionally and vigorously distance themselves from an anachronistic understanding of their place as petty-bourgeois craftsmen and instead identify first and foremost as workers who solve concrete problems through deeply creative acts. This allyship could be one of vocal support, but it could also manifest itself in interdisciplinary alliances that would fundamentally shift power balances between labor and capital. For the design disciplines, this means joining the former against the latter.

In the field of architecture, for example, a current system of ostensible checks and balances exists to separate construction (labor), architecture (design), and development/owner (capital) from each other. Though the three are oft imagined as coequal, the reality is that architecture finds itself most antagonistic to its most historical ally, construction, and almost always acts on behalf of the owner. In essence, design is pitted against labor and made sympathetic to capital, which has not always been the case. This should not surprise anyone, as capital, especially through the real estate industry, has become so powerful in the twenty-first century that architecture finds itself compelled to bend to its will, even if it is not conscious of it. However, since buildings are very much grounded in a localized material reality, from conception to construction, this imbalance of power is a possible source of reform.

The same can be said for the designers of mass-produced goods, as the distance from the production of things (often in other countries) reinforces a faux proximity to the owner class. Because they are embedded in larger and more complex production chains, the process of reorientation would require a much stronger and more systemic political will. However, this makes it a concrete place to start. Aware of the power of the design ethics, these alternative values are the ones that should be pursued if designers are intent on building a world of universal human flourishing, or at the very least making the world a better place through their ability to solve problems for others.

If we instead seek true creative agency, or at least the universal potential of it, design as practiced under capitalism must be critiqued as ruthlessly as the more visible sources of exploitation. Maslow's Hierarchy of Needs provides an intuitive spectrum of this dichotomy: physiological needs (food, water, shelter) and safety needs (employment, health, etc.) on the "bottom," and self-actualization (full-potential including creative acts) on the "top."[63] Joining broader social movements would allow for a focus on addressing the bottom needs and conceptualize them as most important in terms of immediacy, but with an eventual goal of self-actualization for all.

If the eventual places of agency and self-actualization have gone unchallenged, privy only to elites or at use for conspicuous consumption and leisure, they will perpetuate their unique form of creative exploitation. Design, with its special form of imagination, the likes of which Marx and others have revered, has a key role to play in solving the enormously complex crises of our time; it can either continue to be a commodity of a privileged few or a service for people. The next section of this book attempts to build a blueprint for the raising of such a class consciousness.

PART 2

Class Consciousness

> Whatever we do, we are supposed to do for the sake of "making a living"; such is the verdict of society, and the number of people, especially in the professions who might challenge it, has decreased rapidly. The only exception society is willing to grant is the artist, who, strictly speaking, is the only "worker" left in a laboring society.
> —HANNAH ARENDT, *THE HUMAN CONDITION*

Design as Work

We have now arrived at an understanding of the two primary barriers within design professions toward a class consciousness that aligns with worker-centric forms of organization such as unions: creativity and professionalism.[1] These two forces combine in a unique way to consistently deflect movements away from collective action and perpetually toward individualism. When presented with the fact that they make little money compared to other professionals, designers are quick to fall back on their fabricated form of status propped up by misleading notions of (unproductive) creativity and its manifestations through disciplinary privilege. On the other hand, when asked why they haven't unionized or why they don't identify with the working class, the gates of professionalism are quick to close, with designers emphasizing an elevated position based on credentials, education, and technical abilities. These also combine to resist understanding exploitation in economic terms, associating the word with only the basest of working conditions; how can a professional be exploited? A third force, that of history, also plays a part, as older design disciplines such as architecture face a long-standing precedent that does not include a trade union movement, a fact that easily morphs into mythology. Even with the strongest rational arguments for unionization, these multiple faces of anti-class consciousness have proved a strong enough barrier thus far.

In order to develop effective means for subverting both the potency of creative consciousness and the existing professional class-status consensus, along with their intertwined history, it is important to underscore that while these conceptions might *feel* real, they operate as a form of ideology. Even though in many cases such conceptions do influence how people see themselves and others, and even influence how individuals relate socially to others through forms of gatekeeping, they simultaneously undermine not only the ability for individuals to understand themselves as exploited but also that they are part of a larger network of capital, a prerequisite for the reformation (or abolition) of such a system. Exploitation, then, is the first component of a new class consciousness for contemporary designers.

In the *Communist Manifesto*, Marx's historical diagnosis adds a layer that facilitates the movement toward this new ideation: "The lower middle class, the small manufacturer, the shop-keeper, the artisan, the peasant, all these fight against the bourgeoisie, to save from extinction their existence as fractions of the middle class. They are, therefore, not revolutionary, but conservative."[2] Awkwardly sandwiched between the proletariat and the bourgeoisie, those in this "class" are fighting on two fronts, against the proletariat through closure and credentialism and against the bourgeoisie, in the form of wealthy clients, for cheaper contracts and relevant work.

Here we might draw a parallel between what Marx called artisans and design professionals, though it is not a perfect correlation. For some, the categorization is a strong fit, such as a furniture designer, shoemaker, or web-based freelancer, as these designers are in control of their production process and are not owners of other labor, only their own. However, the class-based reality for most designers is not aligned with the artisan but with the factory worker via their economic relationship to production. Even so, the pull toward cultural identification with the artisan remains a strong one, with a studio-based educational ethics inscribing a strong independent ethos among designers. Further, during this crucial time of development, the idealized model of success presented to students is not that of a worker but of the artisan, or petty-bourgeoisie, an independent maker who is free to engage in unencumbered creative pursuits. Regardless, there is no doubt that designers still operate in this "conservative" milieu today; unionization is a fledgling effort in design industries, evidenced by architectural workers only recently forming the first private sector union in over a century.[3] One hundred and fifty years after Marx made the observation, we are hardly much further from the past in our present, with design professionals viewing themselves primarily as "privileged" servants to their clients' interests.

If Marx characterizes such actors as inherently individualistic and conservative, and creative consciousness acts to reinforce these traits, is it possible to engender a new movement, asking design professionals to both accept and reject qualities inherent to their identity? Though he has positioned artisans in the awkward intermediary space between proletariat and bourgeoisie, the shift in consciousness can begin with an earlier observation in the *Manifesto:* "The bourgeoisie has stripped of its halo every occupation hitherto honoured and looked up to with reverent awe. It has converted the physician, the lawyer, the priest, the poet, the man of science, into paid wage-labourers."[4] The modern, professionalized, over-credentialed designer is no different. Therefore, a simple recognition of reality, a real understanding of what it means to be a wage-laborer, is the first step toward the demystification of creative consciousness.

To be a wage-laborer, then, is to be exploited.[5] While many have debated the nature of productive work and who *really* constitutes a worker, for sociologist Erik Olin Wright the dichotomy is clear: "In capitalism the central class relation is the capital/labor relation and this determines two class locations, capitalists and workers."[6] Wright also includes the additional category of the petty-bourgeoisie, but he qualifies that they are "neither exploiter nor exploited" since they do not require the labor of others.[7] While this certainly applies to some designers, especially those who are self-employed, and, of course, *ideologically* many identify with this group, here we are concerned with the actual material conditions in which a vast majority are hired by others and can hence be considered *workers*. Wright expands the definition of workers, folding in "skilled" workers, a term we would use today to describe professional designers: "Both skilled and unskilled workers occupy working-class locations insofar as they do not own or control means of production and must sell their labor power in order to obtain their livelihood, but they vary the amount of one specific resource, skill."[8]

Once class position has been identified, it is important to note that though wage workers are exploited, not all forms of exploitation are the same. According to Wright, there are three primary principles that when combined in a particular way lead to a distinct definition of exploitation: inverse interdependent welfare (the dependency of the worker on a wage for survival), exclusion, and appropriation.[9] When the first two manifest in any given social situation, we have "nonexploitative economic oppression," which is distinct from exploitation itself. A quintessential example would be the colonization of Native Americans in the United States, since their domination was not dependent on extracting surplus-value resulting in direct material gains for their oppressors but rather a forced removal from such desired resources.[10] Although we should not minimize this in any way, we should note that it is more harmful than exploitation *and* necessary, especially historically. For the practice of exploitative labor, it is helpful in clearly defining what the latter means for design workers today.[11]

If designers, then, are going to "wake up" from the slumber of the unconscious aspects of creative consciousness, they must understand that "exploitation depends upon the appropriation of labor effort,"[12] meaning that their boss directly and *materially* benefits from their own labor, and is decidedly dependent on it. In other words, if all the designers in a given office decided to leave their computers, their bosses, even if gifted designers themselves, would no longer be able to support their own livelihood as they are most likely unfamiliar with the software necessary to produce their services. And, even if they are, they do not possess enough hands to reproduce what their staff can do in the same amount of time. As Wright critically observes, "Because human beings are conscious agents, not robots, they always retain significant levels of real control over their expenditure of effort."[13] Convincing them to realize this and to act upon it is really the task at hand.

What, then, will designers do when confronted with a "newly" available consciousness? Will they bend toward the human, or toward the machine?

A New Alignment

It is not without irony that our original theoretician of consciousness, Georg Lukács, might, if not for the previous analysis, also assume the role of our fiercest critic:

> The question of consciousness may make its appearance in terms of the objectives chosen or in terms of action, as for instance in the case of the petty bourgeoisie.... In all decisions crucial for society its actions will be irrelevant and it will be forced to fight for both sides in turn but always without consciousness. In so doing its own objectives—which exist exclusively in its own consciousness—must become progressively weakened and increasingly

divorced from social action. Ultimately they will assume purely ideological forms. The petty bourgeoisie will only be able to play an active role in history as long as these objectives happen to coincide with the real economic interests of capitalism.[14]

Lukács is justifiably skeptical about the political capabilities of the petty-bourgeoisie and the kind of work-based identity they inspire, as evidenced by the false hopes of individual liberation that many designers chase. Content to dream in their "own consciousness," actually manifested in the delirious slumber of creative consciousness, contemporary design professionals have remained in the realm of ideological abstraction, circling around "new" theories, forms, and frivolous methods of making rather than speaking to the immediate needs of everyday people.[15] As such, we might be tempted to definitively label their interests as that of the artisan and petty-bourgeoisie, as this is how they have acted for much of their history. Marx shares a similarly pessimistic view of this group, underscoring their "conservative" and not "revolutionary" tendencies.

Further, if viewed through the Weberian lens of *status*, there is little doubt that contemporary designers have confirmed Luckás's and Marx's fears, leveraging their privileged positions and orienting their *preferred* sense of social relations toward those associated with the petty-bourgeoisie. Obsessing over minor details, distinguishing themselves through style and small-batch artisanal craftsmanship, and generally eschewing popularized, "dull" matters of the masses, they have continually leaned on credentialed enclosure and an inward turn toward esoteric matters. Weber, among many others, sees another reason to distance this group from its revolutionary potential, noting, "Quite generally, among privileged status groups there is a status disqualification that operates against the performance of common physical labor."[16] Hence there are not only ideological and aesthetic reasons to separate such a group, but typological reasons. However, the stakes of stagnating in such a position are certainly high. Just as workers reach consciousness through knowledge of themselves as a commodity, we might miss the opportunity for a new awareness of the designer that *"brings about an objective structural change in the object of knowledge."*[17]

Fortunately, there is another option. Returning to Wright's holistic class analysis, one that does not draw distinctions between skilled and unskilled labor, or manual and physical, there is an alternative path for designers ensnared in the metastasized condition of the petty-bourgeois. Rather than leveraging their privileged position to distance themselves from their "inferiors," designers might *actively choose* to understand their social position through the lens of *exploitation*, removing the ideological shroud of the petty-bourgeoisie and actively joining the collective consciousness of the worker. In other words, just as Lukács emphasizes the necessity of the proletariat to understand itself through the structural categorization of a commodity, designers can do the same through exploitation.

Borrowing the most effective elements of Weber's analysis, and reframing them with a deep understanding of exploitation, Wright provides an effective theory to help break through this conceptual roadblock, but he also highlights the political implications of such a realignment: "Because workers always retain some control over the expenditure of effort and diligence, they have a capacity to resist their exploitation; and because capitalists need workers, there are constraints on the strategies available to capitalists to counter this resistance."[18] The myths explored previously obscure an awareness of the power of workers, pushing designers to maximize their efforts for an ever-moving standard, whether aesthetic or functional. Bending to the will of "creativity," they operate at the expense of forms of agency that can address the impoverishment of their condition. In this kind of labor-centric consciousness, designers, acting as workers, could have an increased capacity to affect change within their workplaces, and perhaps beyond.

However, one cannot resist exploitation, and subsequently make change, if one is not aware that it exists: "Exploitation thus entails a specific kind of duality: conflicting material interest plus a real capacity for resistance."[19] This is in stark contrast to the pessimism of Marx and Lukács, who would rather sideline designers and other like professionals in anticipation of a movement of the true proletariat. Wright's analysis instead provides us with a framework for the beginnings of revolutionary change in a work context that is far more complex, due to specialization and technology, than it was in the nineteenth century. Allowing for traditionally conceived productive workers, Wright's inclusive definition of perspective invites workers of all skills and abilities to direct their dissatisfaction not toward each other but to those at the head of exploitation itself: the owner class.

Even before the proliferation of complexity in work during the twentieth and twenty-first-centuries, there is a model for conceiving of design in a different light, that of the socialist craftsman William Morris. A gifted designer and artisan, Morris could have been content to provide his service to an exclusive few, disregarding the real conditions of his fellow citizens. However, he chose to center much of his thinking and writing on others, being chiefly concerned with the *quality* of workers' lives during his time. Writing to define work as something that should be worth valuing, Morris argued: "Thus worthy work carries with it the hope of pleasure in rest, the hope of the pleasure in our using what it makes, *and the hope of pleasure in our daily creative skill*. All other work but this is worthless; it is slaves' work—mere toiling to live, that we may live to toil."[20] This sharp distinction echoes Marx's call "From each according to his ability, to each according to his needs," one that does not distinguish between certain work as productive and other work as not, or appropriate for revolutionary movements versus that which is comfortably bourgeois. Rather, if not owners, we are *all* workers who must insist on a right to dignified, truly creative work.

Further, Morris not only succinctly expressed the holistic frustration of designers within an increasingly industrialized economic situation, he also was keen to note the reality of who makes such designs possible in the context of our built environment:

> Nor must you forget that when men say popes, kings, and emperors built such and such buildings, it is a mere way of speaking. You

look in your history-books to see who built Westminster Abbey, who built St Sophia at Constantinople, and they tell you Henry III, Justinian the Emperor. Did they? Or rather, men like you and me, handicraftsmen, who have left no names behind them, nothing but their work?[21]

Here we have the explicit call for historians to not attribute great works of architecture to single men, deceptively following the tired individual genius model, but rather the countless men, and today we should say people at large, whose hours of *collective* labor made possible such great works. As we have discussed, this is no different than any other designed object; whether it be a shoe, chair, building or website, it is not possible, even in the most idyllic of artisanal situations that rely on materials no doubt sourced through collective and likely expropriated labor, to design and make something without the labor of others.[22]

Today, our work of shifting consciousness from one dominated by "creativity" to one equally centering labor must also have its sight on the horizon of an actual expression of such a new consciousness; otherwise we will remain in the sphere of ideology rather than a new material alignment. Most simply, this work can manifest as architectural workers, for example, seeing themselves as just that: not as miniature versions of their clients, *petty-bourgeois*, but actors laboring in solidarity with those lauded by Morris who *actually* make conceptual designs a physical reality, the construction workers. This form of solidarity should not just remain in spirit as mentioned, since construction workers are some of the most historically well-organized labor in the United States, routinely better compensated than architects and designers involved in the same projects.[23] As such, the construction industry provides a strong precedent for organizing workers in the same industry, architects. They are now afforded the opportunity to relate to workers in a new way, cutting through barriers developed through years of false consciousness and cultural stereotypes. The implications of such an alliance transcend immediate material benefits for workers as well, with the potential for political alliances with the award of state-funded projects, for example, with architectural and construction unions demanding that projects funded with tax-payer dollars must utilize unionized labor across the board. Outside of the United States, such as in Scandinavia, where union density is between 50 and 80 percent, and in other parts of Europe range from 22 to 29 percent, workers are able to leverage their broad representation in other industries to create ripple effects in many parts of the economy through coordinated demonstrations and cross-sector strikes.[24]

An alignment between architects and construction workers is an obvious expression of a newly developed consciousness, and in the next section we will explore historic and contemporary precedents of designers who eschewed the comforts of ideological aspirations toward the owning-class and instead pursued real, material alliances with the working class. Further, not only have methods of production evolved dramatically since Marx's and Morris's time, but the material interests, and the powerful effect of those interests, is also too impactful to wait for future action. With a hand in shaping the built environment, and a special capacity to envision unique possibilities for complex challenges, designers have been sidelined in the fight against exploitation for too long.

Historical and Contemporary Precedents

As we have seen, there are deeply entrenched motivations, both historical and ideological, for designers to continue the path of individually reinforced bourgeois values, idealizing the nostalgic notion of the individual craftsperson pursuing their vision. The origins of this self-conception are material, and hence real. However, the designers practicing in the twenty-first century, if honest about the conditions in which they operate, should admit such ways of working are idealistic and outdated. From the ever-expanding limits of capital, to increasingly complex buildings and objects that necessitate analogous forms of technological specialization, today's designers find themselves caught between an anachronistic past that has a strong pull, and an uncertain future that sends them returning to the safe grounding of the artisan.

However, designers today should not be so reticent to embrace a new beginning. While painful, a sober reflection on the reality of their material conditions can eventually lead to a newfound position of strength within their own disciplines. Though it will be difficult, and might be seen as a sign of weakness, to admit that the days of strong craft-based knowledge are gone forever, a realignment has the potential to not only return designers to a base level of security but to position them alongside other actors and movements that can begin to address some of our most pressing issues, which threaten the livelihoods of us all.

We can now begin to move from the theoretical to the concrete, examining both past and contemporary examples of labor movements that have centered creativity in their own praxis, providing insights particularly relevant to designers. Further, by examining such overlapping currents, we might be able to articulate a new kind of labor movement that leverages the strong history of workers who have fought for and achieved real wins. Designers, as new members of the workers' movement, can bring their own skills and problem-solving in order to move past existing barriers that have historically blocked labor in the United States.

Before examining contemporary movements, there is a historic one that is valuable for any practitioner who regularly utilizes technology to effectively perform their work. Designers of all stripes use software almost exclusively in the twenty-first-century economy in order to carry out their visions. From architects with BIM (Building Information Modeling) software like Revit, to website designers with Python and other scripting languages, to graphic designers who use the near universal programs that Adobe rents through subscription services, designers are using more software than manual methods of production, and even if they use the latter, no serious proposal can be delivered to the contractor or factory through hand sketches. In other words, the path of production runs through the technological.

While some software overlaps, and often designers utilize technology and software specific to their practice, what is nearly universal is the overwhelming lack of control in the development of such methods of production. First, designers are locked out of ownership through predatory subscription models of companies like Autodesk and Adobe, unable to own such crucial tools to their trade, unthinkable in the age of pen and paper. But perhaps more crucially, they are barred from participating in the *design and development* of those tools. Historically, of course, this might have been less important, as there would have been ample access to various forms of paper, pencils, and ink, and the difference between these tools were negligible or not significant enough to seriously affect outputs. Regardless, one could walk into an art store and exercise agency in the choice of medium necessary for production.

The situation for contemporary designers operating in the digital age could not be more different. Instead of finding themselves browsing the aisles for their favorite acrylic paint, they are forcibly handed software from a limited number of companies. The power and effectiveness of such methods of production should not be understated; one piece of today's creative software contains more "products" than any physical store could offer, comprising increasingly accurate simulacrums of various lead weights for pencils and an uncanny selection of textures and widths for brushes, for example.

This overabundance can create a false sense of satisfaction, akin to a sugar-rush provided from a Times Square candy store, simultaneously hyper-efficient and anything but. Here, one cannot help but be reminded of Morris's prescient critique that workers, during industrialization, had "begun to transform . . . into an enormous stock of human machines . . . who were not asked to think, paid to think, or allowed to think."[25] Many designers today would balk at such a notion, but it is difficult to argue that much of the material intelligence of manual craftsmanship has been usurped by our most familiar machine, the computer. While there are many concerns with the ontology of the use of the technology itself, here we want to focus on the source of such power forms of production.

The relationship to production and the development of technology is central to not just designers, but all workers. Well into the twenty-first century, the computer is no longer the central source of anxiety in relation to technological development—artificial intelligence (AI) and automation occupy much of the ongoing discourse within the labor movement. While most of these developments seem to appear out of thin air, or even inevitable, many are beginning to question the speed and necessity of such a dramatic shift in the way we work. The most visceral example of this was the 2023 writers' and actors' strikes in Hollywood, with AI a central issue to the fraught negotiations.[26] Architecture, however, like most sectors of the building industry, has been comparatively slow to adopt serious AI technology, though those designers more versed with contemporary software have made AI central to their practice, whether intentional or not. Most popular conversation is limited to the ways in which AI can produce more design options, more quickly, while others pursue familiar narratives of human-labor replacement, a popular topic since the rise of computers. Regardless of the speculation, we should still be impressed, and maybe unnerved, by the actual progression of architectural production since the widespread adoption of computer-aided drawing (CAD) in professional practice over the last forty years. Such whiplash, while increasing productivity and efficiency, has also had its share of anxiety and frustration. Similarly, video game designers, for example, are producing works that spectacularly border on the real and even compete with the storytelling capabilities of traditional film, achieving cinematographic complexity unimaginable in the twentieth century.

In order to fully realize the weight of the issues surrounding digital production and technology, it is worth briefly summarizing its recent history through the material example of architectural production, which overlaps in its use of software and computing techniques with other design industries. Beginning with an initial technological paradigm shift of the use of computers, architectural production increased its speed and productivity overnight while largely maintaining the same operational workflow, that of individually developed drawings that were laboriously compiled to make a digital drawing set. In this case, the "author" is still entirely responsible both for the actual drawing, as well as the painstaking coordination between all drawings the computer viewed more as a productive supplement rather than a consequential actor itself.

The transition to BIM, beginning in the 1990s, has been more turbulent: instead of starting with a blank "page" and developing a drawing from nothing, the entire process has been reversed through the progressive application of individual lines and geometry. Now, the "user" ("author" feels less appropriate in this case, and is in fact what Autodesk refers to us as) constructs a 3D model which the software then uses to generate drawings, all with essentially the click of a button. Though these drawings need many rounds of revisions, it is worth underscoring that the initial drawing itself, at least the majority of the geometry necessary for the final product, is "generated" through a process that does not involve the user at all.

While many might find these developments unremarkable, or simply inevitable, especially in the context of day-to-day demands from clients, always speeding up themselves, in the historical context of architectural production, they are nothing but radical. With origins nearly a thousand years ago, manual drafting has all but been erased in the span of less than half a century.[27] Further, the adoption of such rapidly developed technology has been uneven, as many schools primarily work in the "first" epoch of CAD, and some still even teach manual drafting, while few if no offices use the latter, many the former, and many more have adopted BIM exclusively. This tension in the relationship to technology and craft is a topic that deserves further exploration, but the broader point still remains: technology is developing incredibly quickly, and the source of such development is ambiguous at best, with little consensus of what qualifies as necessary or best practice for those who actually produce architectural work.

Though within the architectural community there is much debate regarding whether such developments are "good" or "bad," the reality is this: architectural *workers* have had no involvement, and the situation is only accelerating, with designers of all stripes facing the same reality. Each year it feels as though we are handed new updates, or entirely new pieces of software, with no understanding of why or how they came to be. Though we might feel helpless now, we can look to the strikes in Hollywood not just for their relevance in relation to the use of AI, but more important, for what makes their resistance so effective: *collective action through strong unions.*

Well before the emergence of AI, many social critics had noted the contradictory development in the technologicalization of work, carrying a quality of increasing educational and intellectual demand while simultaneously producing worsening working conditions.[28] Predicting the constraining effects of technology and automation, these analyses capture the growing sense that automation would deeply affect not just physical working conditions but also the mental well-being of workers; AI seems prime to significantly worsen the latter.

In our ostensibly privileged professions, through our adeptness in utilizing such technology, designers might still feel in control of their methods of production. However, companies like Autodesk and Adobe, which are essentially monopolies in the realm of design production, ultimately have similar intentions as the production companies in Hollywood. Autodesk is currently teaming up with venture capital firms to develop software that "manage their drawing sets more efficiently."[29] Though the relationship between screen actors and AI took up much of the attention during the strike, the productive struggle itself is the result of a deeper underlying relationship, a debate over who gets to make the most consequential decisions regarding the use of technology. In other words, without such effective organizing, actors and writers would be subject to CEOs' desires without input.

Concretely, writers in the 2023 strike achieved not only increased pay and job security, but equally important "regulations for the use of artificial intelligence (AI) on MBA-covered projects."[30] Such protections for workers would never have been secured without the backing of unions and intersectional solidarity between multiple labor groups. Similarly, auto workers, in their own strikes, secured agreements from GM to fold electric battery plants into the national contract, a significant win in the fight over worker involvement in fast-growing and critically important EV development. And in our negotiations at Bernheimer Architecture, we were able to include language in our contract that recognized the dignity of human-centered work and design, created avenues for employee participation in decisions surrounding technology and software, and also specifically protected employees from digital monitoring. Real participation in the actual development of production will require a different strategy, one that an obscure Swedish experiment can provide.

UTOPIA

Although it may seem utopian in today's climate, creating an alliance between labor and the companies that develop software is possible, and one such project provides a powerful model for doing so.[31] During the 1970s and 1980s, the UTOPIA Project, founded in Sweden, centered worker involvement in the development of technology. The program's goal, as technology scholar Robert Howard explains, was to help unions translate their social values regarding job skills, quality of work, and quality of products into new computer hardware and software for the journalism and printing industry:

> Nowhere has union activism on these issues gone further than in Scandinavia. Beginning in Norway in the late 1960s, and extending to Denmark and Sweden over the next decade, technical specialists from government-funded institutions such as the Norwegian Computing Center in Oslo and the Swedish Center for Working Life joined unionists to study the effects of new technology on work and to formulate realistic union strategies to address them. These "action research" projects spread throughout Scandinavia in metalworking shops, chemical refineries,

railroad repair shops, insurance offices, retail stores, and newspaper offices. They quickly took on the form of a popular-education movement. Workers began to understand technology as something they might be able to influence—just like other aspects of working life.[32]

In this way, participants hoped to shape the impacts of new technology on workers before it ever reached the shop floor—an unthinkable method of development in the United States.

Although it did not last long, encompassing the years between 1981 and 1986, the UTOPIA Project's effects were long-lived. Envisioned as a development and training program, it specifically centered on newly emerging text and image processing in the graphic industries. Forgoing traditional schisms between work "classifications," two disparate groups were consulted for the project: top-level "work-efficiency" experts, system designers, computer scientists, and other technocrats alongside representatives from labor: union leaders, activists, and workers themselves, ranging from printers to lithographers, all representing a wide swath of skilled labor in the newspaper and printing industries.

Visiting UTOPIA's lab in Sweden in 1985, Howard observed a scene that might have been more common in a research department in any high-tech company: an individual user completing typical tasks in front of a computer screen while a team of scientists recorded observations regarding the work. In other words, the effort was collaborative, even from the scientific observation stage. What makes this model so powerful is the reversal of relations in the development of the technology itself:

> Seeing the computer as a tool also implies a different understanding of the process by which new technical systems are developed. Most designers create a highly abstract model of a work process, and then try to incorporate that model into new computer hardware and software. Often, workers using the system end up as little more than passive objects of automation. UTOPIA's goal

was to put the centuries-old traditions and occupational knowledge of printers at the center of the design process. Workers would play an active role in determining what kind of technology they needed and how it could support them in their work.[33]

It is this *centering* that is crucial to the vitality of the entire project, an inversion of typical social relations within the workplace.

This model might be enticing for software designers who, according to technologist Jaron Lanier, suffer from the problem of "lock-in," a process of design decisions "freezing" the further development of software. This process limits the future development of any other software, which is confined by the overbearing decisions of past models and schematics.[34] Though today software designers might feel unable to imagine an alternative scenario, through a strong unionization effort and a program like UTOPIA they could realize a tangible means for designing how they design. Not only do they have an interest in designing the software they themselves use, they are also the closest in proximity to the company owners and billionaires who have an outsized role in shaping the technology responsible for administering capitalism as we know it. With such a strong working knowledge of the technology all workers are subject to, unionized software designers could be at the forefront of addressing our broken relationship with the tech industry, bringing the design of technology from the few to the many.

UTOPIA was created out of an unusual set of circumstances: the government primarily funded it, strong unions backed it, companies were unusually cooperative, and radical scientists from the 1960s were eager for experimentation, all of whom had interests in the success of the project beyond profit-making. However, considered within the context of other models, it becomes a key precedent in envisioning and organizing radical worker movements.

Car Production Reorganized

Auto workers, too, can help us bridge the gap between the radical

Scandinavian experiments of the past with the relatively radical reemergence of American labor organizing today. Traditionally not viewed as "creative" labor by bourgeois economists and mainstream sociologists, the intricate work of assembling cars is anything *but* uncreative, a prime example of the definition of creativity that centers on productiveness. This is especially evident in the workers' continual confrontation with the owner class, a model that designers should study closely.

During the 1980s, labor experimentation in Sweden was not limited to the UTOPIA Project; similarly, the auto industry was seeking ways to unite state, private, and labor interests in new ways, with the most innovative thinking unsurprisingly coming from labor. In particular, the Swedish company Volvo, responding to labor market pressures, embarked on a radical reconception of the assembly line in a new manufacturing plant in Uddevalla in 1989. Since the plant was forced to shut down during an economic crisis a few years later, much of the success of the project has been buried in contrarian critics conflating broader economic forces with the decisions of the workers behind the implementation of the new scheme. Professor of Industrial Management Christian Berggren's research has, however, demonstrated the opposite: the new organization was not only beneficial mentally to workers, but more effective and productive than traditional Fordist models.[35] As such, ignoring the detractors who seek to uphold the visions of Fordism and Taylorism, the Uddevalla model can provide effective guidance for workers seeking more meaningful participation in the design and implementation of their means of production.

Addressing concerns of both a tight labor market that necessitated innovations to attract workers, as well as aging modes of technical production, Volvo created a "wholly new concept" in the sphere of assembly production of vehicles, audaciously referred to as "the death of the assembly line."[36] The organization of the plant was an interesting spatial issue: gone were the long, snake-like conveyor belts and robotic movements of the workers, a quintessential organization of the division of labor, replaced by a star-shaped dispersion of multiple vehicles undergoing simultaneous construction.[37] One can imagine the psychological uplift provided through such a spatial organization workers were now able to see the entire process of production in contrast to the linear conveyor belt method that only provides a narrow view of the process.[38]

This novel form of productive organization addressed alienation of the workers in two ways: first, by reconnecting workers to a holistic cycle of labor, which provided both increased mental and physical well-being,[39] and second, by reducing the involvement of management in decision-making regarding conditions of work, an intransigent source of worker dissatisfaction in all workplaces. This latter relationship, between management and workers, is central in workplace struggles because it is managers, in alliance with owners, whose decision-making determines the conditions that primarily produce the forms of alienation that the Uddevalla scheme sought to ameliorate. Braverman was keen to give significant space to this topic in *Labor and Monopoly Capital,* underscoring that machinery is leveraged not to improve worker conditions, as in the case with Uddevalla, but more typically as the "prime means whereby production may be controlled not by the direct producer but by the owners and representatives of capital."[40] In other words, the struggle over the use of machinery, and in our age digital computation, is the struggle over labor itself. Workers at Uddevalla understood that management was not the group willing to initiate any sort of change that directly challenged their forms of control:

> Most of management also had a narrow perspective on the possibilities for reform, even after it had rejected the Kalmar model. In the meantime, innovative engineers and researchers had the opportunity to pursue far more radical alternatives, and, most important, to develop the entirely new support systems (materials handling, technical information structures, and so forth) that would be required by a transformed assembly operation.[41]

While innovation is popularly ascribed to owners, many of the ideas for novel solutions are produced by the workers, those most intimately aware of the intricate processes behind project and product deliveries. When given the opportunity to develop proposals that are unmediated by management concerns, it is no surprise that such "radical" ideas translate to increased productivity and better end results.

Aside from the issue of multiple iterations leveraged through the exploitation of design, management routinely finds other ways to extract surplus labor out of its workforce, and actively stymies attempts from workers to increase their own productivity, address problems more efficiently, and generally determine the direction of their own work. While most workers, like the auto workers, have direct knowledge in the day-to-day operations of their workplaces, management usually neglects this perspective and instead problem-solves through their own limited perspective, hiring and firing more staff or promoting themselves, for example, when the actual answers can be found in the material knowledge of workers. This is what makes the models provided by UTOPIA and Uddevalla so powerful, as they create tangible means for workers to empower *themselves*, developing antidotes to forms of alienation, for example, that they themselves are most familiar with. Central to this conflict between management and workers is a struggle for power and control; for if management were truly interested in increased productivity, they would have an interest in following such precedents.

Similarly, the UAW (United Auto Workers) in twenty-first-century United States, to the surprise of many, resisted the hegemonic control of owners in its own methods of production to win historic contracts for its members. Written off as a weak union, mired in corruption, one that had refused to meaningfully challenge the big auto corporations for years, the election of a new president, Shawn Fain, who promised militancy over complacency, ignited one of the most successful labor struggles in recent memory. Prior to the success in the auto industry, the UAW built off a series of historic strikes and subsequent wins on college campuses across the country, negotiating strong contracts for existing students and faculty, as well as bringing into the union a large number of new members. Concurrently, strikes gripped Hollywood, and actors and writers, in what might be more traditionally understood as "creative" industries, united to defend their own work from economic precarity and encroaching technological domination. Whereas the examples from UTOPIA and Uddevalla provide insights into unique forms of worker control in processes of production, it is not possible to achieve without the backing of strong collective action through unionization. As such, the auto, university, and Hollywood strikes serve as crucial precedents for understanding the power of union density, demonstrating that the only way to bring about actual, impactful changes is through confrontational struggle.

Central to any labor negotiation are issues of economic importance such as wages and working hours, a common thread in all of the above mentioned movements. Auto workers at GM, Ford, and Stellantis won 25 percent raises,[42] faculty at The New School, through a historic strike, won a minimum of 30 percent,[43] and writers gained much needed increases to minimum pay rates and pension contributions.[44] It goes without saying that such impressive gains in compensation, while long overdue, would not be possible without the support of unions who were willing, through the courage of their members, to withhold their labor.

However, the most interesting connection between contemporary strikes and the historic Swedish models is the hinge issue of technology and labor. While each movement brought its own particular interests with respect to technology and production, it was through union density within all industries that real changes could be implemented. In the case of auto workers, the burgeoning Electric Vehicle (EV) market became a central issue in negotiations. While the consensus was that traditional fossil-fuel burning vehicles would remain in the domain of unionized production and the forward-looking EVs would be exempt, negotiators leveraged their strong position to ensure that technological production was aimed toward the future, and hence rational growth was folded into collective bargaining. This also prevented an important political schism, one that would reinforce stereotypes about unions as opposed to progress and change; instead, the UAW ensured that its membership was present in *all* forms of production as the economy transitions from dependence on fossil-fuels.

Hollywood and AI

Similarly, technology was at the heart of the struggle between production companies and writers and actors. Concerned about the encroachment of AI in both writing and acting, workers united to take a stand against surreptitious theft of their intellectual and creative products. For writers, this manifested in the form of machine-learning models that could use previously written scripts in order to produce cheap facsimiles, completely undercutting the human-centered labor behind writing compelling stories and narratives. Although the results were less than impressive, writers could see the eventual end of such a path, with technology progressing to a point in which it would be entirely possible to eliminate all human labor from the writing process. Through confrontational organizing and strong shows of solidarity, writers were able to force companies to concede on their aggressive use of AI, ensuring protections for the use of the labor of writers.[45] Specifically, they forced Hollywood executives to acknowledge the existence of an imbalance of power, only remedied through a strong contract: "The WGA reserves the right to assert that exploitation of writers' material to train AI is prohibited by MBA or other law."[46] Actors too share fears about AI stealing their work, in this case machines able to directly generate digital versions of themselves that were nearly impossible to identify as such. Though both felt in precarious positions, the intersection of writers and actors, seen together on the picket lines for the first time in over half a century, along with their strong unions, created a potent force that production companies could not defeat.[47]

Design industries are not quite in the same place as other historically organized sectors, but it is not difficult to imagine what could be achieved if they were. This model would seem to appeal strongly to those designers whose products of design are digital, such as video game and graphic designers. Although the latter have moved through a historical shift from manual to digital production, much like architects, the former are workers born into an industry that is a direct result of the digital revolution. For example, we are beginning to see video game workers become cognizant of their true class positions, pushing back against crippling management demands during what is known as "crunch-time," leading the way among designers through fast-growing organizing movements.[48] Though each design discipline will need to do the important work of identifying the issues that are particular to its own labor, there is undoubtedly more that unites them than divides them, as seen with the overlapping threads that run through all of the precedents mentioned in this section. Now is the time for designers to understand their inherent strengths and form collective actions, the only effective means for changing the conditions that have wrought their industries. If they do, they might not only reform their own practices but begin to join in addressing the most pressing issues of our time.

Emancipatory Design

Perhaps what is most promising about reinvigorated labor movements is not the traditional contractual wins, but the potential for industries and disciplines to reimagine their transformative potential within society at large. This moment of burgeoning strength is an important one to ensure that our lens is not only narrowly focused but also observing larger trends that are at the root of so many of the problems designers are attempting to mitigate. If not, unions risk falling into a form of insular protectionism, viewed as weakened former allies that only serve traditional notions of productive industries.

Polymath economist Michael Polanyi, writing on class developments leading up to the First Wrold War, emphasized a "double movement," which saw contributory classes fostering social protections, while those pursuing economic liberalism undermined them:

On the other hand, the trading classes had no organ to sense the dangers involved in the exploitation of the physical strength of the worker, the destruction of family life, the devastation of neighborhoods, the denudation of forests, the pollution of rivers, *the deterioration of craft standards*, the disruption of folkways, and the *general degradation of existence including housing and arts*, as well as the innumerable forms of private and public life that do not affect profits.[49]

So far, the critique has been aimed at the status-based alignment of designers, and rightfully so. This work is running up against hundreds of years of complacency, and there is more work to do to continue to dismantle it. However, we shouldn't be mistaken in determining the root cause of such myopia (a weakness in common forms of design criticism): the real forces at the hand of liberal economic policy that initially created the milieu in which such misguided thinking is fostered. At the time "craft standards, housing and the arts" were being eroded, a small "cross-class" alliance, operating outside the realm of capitalistic production, emerged, resisting such destructive efforts:

> Here lay the chance of those classes which were not engaged in applying expensive, complicated, or specific machines to production. Roughly, to the landed aristocracy and the peasantry fell the task of safeguarding the martial qualities of the nation which continued to depend largely on men and soil, while the laboring people, to a smaller or greater extent, became representatives of the common human interests that had become homeless. But at one time or another, each social class stood, even if unconsciously, for interests wider than its own.[50]

Contemporary designers are also in a similarly privileged position; honing unique critical thinking skills and an ability to envision alternative futures, qualities baked into their very work, and simultaneously not restricted to a direct form of exploitation at the hand of capital,⁵¹ they have an advantage that not all workers have in *choosing their class alignment*. According to Polanyi, there is a historical precedent for a new consciousness that can usurp that of the creative, one that stands for the "common human interests" instead of the individual. Marx ultimately shares a similar goal. Even though he was skeptical of the political capacity of the petty-bourgeoisie, the measurement for success in the end is pluralistic: "The real fruit of [the worker's] battles lies, not in the immediate result, but in the *ever-expanding union of the workers*."⁵²

We might also begin to envision not just an expanded working class, but an expanded notion of *design itself*. Although designers are incredibly proficient at imagining what is not yet, a skill that "distinguishes the worst architect from the best of bees,"⁵³ they have been satisfied with ceasing their labor efforts there, socially aspiring to the material qualities of the capitalist class, an alliance that without doubt has exacerbated the deterioration and degradation of the built environment that Polanyi speaks to.

But what if design were to participate in the *conversation* and subsistence of the home, for example, not just its material shape?⁵⁴ What if it were to forgo joining "capital in exploiting common labor" as observed by W. E. B. Du Bois, and instead forges new alliances that elevate all workers?⁵⁵ What if it were to turn away from capital altogether and seek to integrate and cultivate, rather than protect its own interest and neglect the border ecology environment it consumes?⁵⁶ These are just some of the most pressing issues of twenty-first-century capitalism. But before designers can effectively address them, they must, after confronting the ideological version of a creative consciousness that holds them back, pivot toward the more expansive goal of integrating with other causes, joining the efforts for emancipation.⁵⁷ Perhaps then they might finally "play an active role in history."

PART 3

Together We Build

> The worst walls are never the ones you find in your way. The worst walls are the ones you put there—you build yourself. Those are the high ones, the thick ones, the ones with no doors.
> —URSULA K. LE GUIN, *LANGUAGE OF THE NIGHT*

Many professions have been absent from the most important social movements of the past half-century.[1] From antiwar to feminist struggle, to Black Liberation and militant union strikes, professional workers are often nowhere to be seen, especially designers. However, they might be emerging now from their slumber, marching in more protests than in the past; perhaps this is evidence of shaking the confines of creative consciousness. Yet the uptick in participation is marginal, and it is certainly not widely reported. While important for developing a resistance to the exploitation that all designers face, protests and unionization efforts can easily remain trapped. In that state, such movements exist as nothing more than a form of gatekeeping and protectionism that seeks to exclusively foster the well-being of its own citizens, an ineffectual embrace of zero-sum thinking, gaining wins at the expense of others. The evidence of such enclosure is stark: two out of every five emerging architects are women, only 21 percent are Hispanic or Latino, and 7 percent are Black or African American. The data for licensed architects is even bleaker, with 66 percent comprising white men.[2] Graphic design, for example, which has a more balanced gender split (approximately 50-50), is even *less* racially diverse: 77 percent of workers are white, while only 9 percent are Asian and 5 percent Black.[3]

Though there is work being done to ameliorate the lack of representation within design disciplines, a tired approach from the professional establishment will, as a best-case scenario, create a more diverse group of privileged workers, with management dictating those portions of labor that are diverse. Worse yet, a performative "lean-in" type of representation might emerge that does little to change the root causes of such inequities.[4] Further, it is not just in areas of class, gender, and race that design has been absent. All of the factors above are intertwined with the climate crisis, its schemes and inventions leading to the making of environmentally unsound products and buildings, as well as a cycle dependent on unsustainable rates of growth through proliferating commodification. Attempts to rectify these problems have been largely unsuccessful.[5] It is for this reason we must look beyond traditional pursuits of performative diversification and sustainability and instead seek to address problems at the intersection of multiple issues.

Though design is culpable of maintaining narrow interests, this lack of reciprocity cuts both ways, as social movements have either unintentionally, through intense focus on the immediate issues at hand, ignored professions or treated them as antagonists impeding real progress. While there is little doubt that this has been true, a new paradigm is needed, as the scale of crises we face is growing at an unprecedented rate, with entrenched elected officials doing little to shift a status quo that protects the interest of the ruling class above all. Accordingly, if we seek to make real structural alterations across all aspects of our political economy, there is no more time for isolated camps seeking to effect change individually. It is worth underscoring at the beginning of this section a potential method for achieving this, what I refer to as "disciplinary synthesis" as argued for by John Bellemy Foster. This is a call for sociology to "extend into the ecological realm" and for ecology to do the same. And further, that without each other, both are "incapable of dealing with the contemporary crisis of the earth—a crisis which has its source and its meaning ultimately in society itself."[6] This is true of any cause; while design needs the critical analysis and invigorating energy of social movements, social movements need the imaginative thinking and problem-solving capabilities of design. In this way, the unionization efforts within design disciplines can be seen as a building block toward the larger goal of broader social and political change, an integral component of the project to radically transform our institutions to those that do not merely serve the few, but the needs of all. This last part of the book is by no means a comprehensive analysis of the work of other movements, or even a sufficient attempt at fully understanding such important work; rather, it is a conceptual sketch, not demarcated or artificially divided, but made of ideas woven together in an aspirational new form of solidarity that, in the words of Architectural Workers United's campaign slogan, "Together We Build."

So far, the examples presented here have been mainly of traditional labor. Though we might debate if designers and journalists are as productive as, say, the Swedish auto workers, they both are "free" to sell their labor in order to earn a wage, hence qualify straightforwardly as exploited. However, other forms of labor that have been traditionally excluded from such definitions have just as much to teach us about not only work, but what it means to be creative in the sense of *tekhné*, and any movement that aims to seriously challenge entrenched forms of power will need an alliance between both of these crucial groups. This final section will begin with three thinkers whose work, considered collectively, intersects at the juncture of feminism, race, labor, and design.

If we are to investigate the intersection of gender and labor, there is perhaps no better place to begin than with the work of Nancy Fraser.[7] Consistently seeking alternatives to entrenched conceptions and unhelpful binaries, Fraser's work spans a wide range of cultural, philosophical, economic, and political critique. In a recent article, Fraser asks an important question, one that we are attempting to address here: "Why is there no broad coalition of new-New Dealers: trade unionists, unemployed and precarious workers; feminists, ecologists and anti-imperialists; social democrats and democratic socialists?"[8] A helpful concept for beginning to develop an answer is in Fraser's earlier writing on the issue of "redistribution and recognition," the former defined as those issues more familiar to traditional labor movements (economic redistribution through collective unity), and the latter alerting the broader public consciousness to the issues specific to a particular group (cultural prominence through group-based action).[9] This specific framing is helpful because though this work has primarily been concerned with redistribution, its true effectiveness and potential power will come through the type of supplemental model Fraser proposes. As she suggests, the two are often in conflict as one seeks to be widely expansive and the other focused and particular, inhibiting each kind of important work from being fully successful.[10]

Here, according to Fraser, gender exists in the murky space between redistribution and recognition, and as such, serves as the ideal social issue to interrogate our own analysis. Initially, it is easy to conceive it as an issue of redistribution since it relies on "the fundamental division between paid 'productive' labor and unpaid 'reproductive' and domestic labor," the fight being one to end such arbitrary differentiations through the form of closing the pay gap, for example, and folding in unpaid reproductive and social labor into the realm of compensatory labor.[11] However, movements with gender at the center can also be considered those of fights for recognition, as traditional manifestations of masculinity dominate our social spheres, with spaces such as the office subjecting everyone to prescribed rules of behavior that are more likely to be rewarded not just fiscally but culturally.[12] Within the design realm, it is not difficult to find examples of the dual nature of this struggle; architecture has an entrenched "recognition" problem when it comes to gender, and this is amplified within the building industry as a whole, with no space more hostile to non-masculine ideals than the construction site. In product and software design, the rules of "working fast and breaking things" also play into these tropes, with brashness and egotism crowding out other approaches to work. But, as Fraser notes, the two competing values run into each other: "Here, then, is the feminist version of the redistribution-recognition dilemma: how can feminists fight simultaneously to abolish gender differentiation and to valorize gender specificity?"[13]

Fraser suggests two ways of thinking, which seek to not simply work around the margins but to change fundamental structures: transformation and emancipation. Transformation relies on "deep restructuring of relations of production," "deep restructuring of relations of recognition," and "blurs group differentiation."[14] In other words, instead of "affirmation," which calls for recognition but mostly on the surface, commonly known as "identity politics," transformation is an attempt at reorganizing the fundamental structure of the elements that result in the inequities we are concerned with. Importantly, it affirms group identities while simultaneously blurring them through a contemporaneous struggle for economic justice in the form of class antagonisms, primarily through the mechanisms of socialist redistribution.[15] Although it is a difficult balancing act, from the perspective of this analysis, it is vital to maintain as a centering principle, a way to ensure that designers are not simply achieving traditional economic gains in the form of better wages, for example, but also working with others to help transform the underpinnings of an unequal society.

A rare example of feminist-design thinking comes from the architectural collective Matrix, which produced an important manifesto in the 1960s in the form of a field manual that still resonates with many of the issues facing contemporary design, a manual that could be of use in seeking change that is transformative. While Fraser seeks to "deconstruct" through theoretical transformative action, Matrix sought to *reconstruct* the built environment in a way that was in the same spirit of radical reimagining. Central to

Matrix's critique is the observation that most architects do little to understand the needs of those who, in their words, "will actually *use* the buildings" and that the majority of said architects are men.[16] This extends to the building industry at large: it is not just architects who are predominantly men, but also developers and builders, the two ends of the production cycle of a building. The figures, while not quite as dismal as the time Matrix was writing, are still lopsided. Regardless, the exclusionary nature of design at large also means that a narrow range of perspectives is represented in some of the most consequential decision-making that shapes the environment around us. For Matrix, the particular historical moment was an intense reaction to midcentury modernism, the de facto orientation for not just individual buildings, but for the city itself. Inaugurated through important advances in building technology, much of the utopian vision of modernism had gone astray, manifested in cold materials, grossly exaggerated spaces, and a general disregard for human scale. This critique shares much with Jane Jacobs's famous writing on the woes of modern planning, but importantly it incorporates a clearer gender-based perspective. However, the most interesting connection was to the issues plaguing the broader economy, issues that were out of sight for the proponents of such schemes. Drawing a connection between the lack of women involved in design, Matrix explained that "the forms of buildings were influenced by economic and political pressures rather than social needs. . . . Politicians believed that the massive housing problem would be solved by the use of new materials, factory-made components and mass construction of standardized units."[17] Executing design through identifying problems from a predominantly male-centric view, the majority of the traditional workforce, the results of many modernist projects alienated large swaths of the population, their needs neglected. An important concrete example identified by Matrix is the lack of accessible options for strollers when moving through urban environments. Through creating more stroller-friendly designs like ramps and curb cuts, the intention is to provide accessibility for caretakers (predominantly women at the time of their writing), but in practice, accessibility is provided for all, including men returning from business trips with luggage or service workers delivering packages. Overall, the emphasis on social relations is key here; these were the motives behind the big men of the day observing life not from the realities of the everyday, but instead from alienated ideologies, which claimed to solve societal issues but which, in reality, exacerbated many of them.

If Fraser provides a theoretical framework, and Matrix a material critique, then a third necessary element of such an analysis would be one that is oriented toward political action. Activist and theorist Veronica Gago's involvement in the labor demonstrations in Argentina through Ni Una Menos (Not One More) is one such example, that of feminism and labor uniting through concrete action in order to effect change. As is the case in many union environments throughout the globe, the Argentinian union base was male-dominated, with an incredibly conservative definition of labor. But because Argentina already has high union density throughout the country, in Gago's perspective it was the perfect environment to pursue feminist struggles, not in isolation, but in solidarity with traditional labor.

Beginning with the observation made by feminists before her, Gago centers unpaid reproductive and social labor in the intellectual framing of her work. Contrary to most economists that see child-rearing, housework, and other such unpaid labor as "free," Gago demands that we not only conceptually understand that such labor is the backbone of capitalism, but that it can be leveraged to force the proponents of such a mentality to reconsider their position. Additionally, the idea of productivity itself is critiqued, freeing it from its definition in terms of wages. Although this traditional definition is predicated on exploitation, it simultaneously pushes social labor to the margins.[18] In other words, with a strongly unionized labor force the standard in Argentina, the problem of unpaid labor becomes more acute since it is forced to be perpetually framed against well-paid, protected, and "hypermasculine" forms of work. Such a powerful framing can become even stronger, excluding others from participating in the benefits of collectivity.

For Gago, this sets the stage for a necessary alliance with labor, though not one that is merely performative, but transformational. Calling this kind of solidarity "transversal," Gago underscores the importance of each side learning from and sharing themselves in the form of the Other:

> The transversality of the feminist movement finds a very important alliance in the union component, both in terms of mobilization as well as in massiveness and impact. In turn, the strength of the joint action turns union "unity" into a new question, because it exceeds the definition of who is a worker, since they have now achieved the inter-union recognition of popular economy workers, as well as non-unionized workers. By the union's recognition of the production of value of reproductive, community, neighborhood, and precarious tasks, the union limit ceases to be a "fence" that confines work as something exclusively belonging to formal workers, to account for the concealment of other activities that the wage and precarization also exploit. The slogan that emerged from the strike in the midst of the Feminist International—#AllWomenAre Workers—synthesizes this movement.[19]

Our work here operates along similar lines, with the same expansive basis—we are *all* workers. Doing the difficult work of "lowering the fence" around unions and folding in social and reproductive labor in her own context, Gago and her movement ensured that their social actions would transform to become a "feminism of the masses."[20] Concretely, this was best done through leveraging the most effective tool of unions, the withholding of labor through the strike. No longer a tool for the exclusive use of unions, Ni Una Menos organized via the "feminist strike," marching first in 2017 for International Women's Day, eventually mobilizing 800,000 women for the same event in 2018 and 2019. Concurrently, the same organizational methods of the feminist strike were used to fight for the successful legalization of abortion in Argentina in 2020.[21] The broad success of this movement in economic and reproductive spheres is in large part thanks to the united front of labor and feminism.

Unfortunately, like many countries, Argentina is susceptible to the vicissitudes of contemporary neoliberal politics and elected a president who is more than hostile to the vital work Gago has helped lead. Hopefully with such a strong foundation, Ni Una Menos can be at the center of resistance to such destructive political forces. If anything, we here in the United States are familiar enough with similar opposition. In the new millennium, we have been plagued with political instability and stagnation at the hands of two political parties that promise to represent the interests of change but continually fail to deliver. As regular folks do the difficult work of pushing elected officials toward progress for the issues most important to them, facing a complacency that weakens such efforts, those in opposition further erode the possibilities of such change. In the face of such political games, it is easy to feel discouraged.

However, there might still be hope in such an unnerving situation. In the face of oppressive resistance, we can return to Gago's words, ensuring that we continue to "nurture a collective desire to change everything."[22] As those in power continually fail in the context of our two-party system, relying on business-as-usual electoral politics is not enough. Instead, we must embrace collective thinking that seeks to call attention to our most pressing problems, but simultaneously emphasizes the interests of the many rather than the few. Here we might think of the successful efforts to raise the minimum wage across several states at a time of historic inequality, or the surprising success of ballot measures that codify reproductive rights in the deepest of red states. These changes came not from the ideas of the political class of consultants, but from the experience of everyday life for those involved. This echoes our call for designers to turn away from protecting the interests of the owner class and instead engage with those projects that represent the improvement of material conditions for the working class. And, even though these issues Gago calls attention to are traditionally outside of the scope of design, we can underscore the broad thinking of Matrix, which pushes us to understand that nothing is in isolation. And that focusing on the improvement of conditions for one group can coincide with the improvement of all. In other words, every designed thing is influenced by not just the obvious social relations directly involved in its production, but the broader social relations behind its pre- and post-existence.

WE CAN LEARN MUCH ABOUT the history of both race and labor in the United States from W. E. B. Du Bois's *Black Reconstruction in America*. This text is well known for its historical contributions to a deep understanding of the era of Reconstruction, but Du Bois has as much to say about labor, analyzing race through its lens and vice versa. This can be seen in the first two chapters, "The Black Worker" and "The White Worker," respectively. These analyze the different racial conditions of each group, but remarkably, they also emphasize their common connection, that of workers, a message we are in dire need of in light of divisive language surrounding race. Most of the writing is a lamentation on the unseized potential of recognizing this common ground, but nonetheless it is important to center this critical work in any labor movement of the twenty-first century, even if largely forgotten.

Du Bois begins this monumental work with an origin story for the United States, one that offers many clues toward the development of particular kinds, or lack thereof, of class consciousness. Emphasizing the land as central to this narrative, we begin with the Black worker, and two critical observations about their unique character: first, it not only had a foundation in Southern "social structure" but also in Northern industry, and even English production overseas.[23] This situated Black labor in its true historical and spatial position, as not only a regional issue but one that extended throughout the country and even the globe. As such, dominant textile manufacturing centers of the time, the northern United States and England, could not produce their goods without expropriated Black labor. This has further importance in that "the growing exploitation of white labor" in Europe, differentiated from *expropriated* Black labor, directly led to increased immigration to the United States. Here we see the reciprocal relationship between the direct support of dominant capitalist production built implicitly on Black labor and explicitly through white labor, with the latter free in the sense that, while exploited, it still maintained the ability to move to a different job and country in the pursuit of a better life, at the expense of Black labor, which had no such privileges. This is the inherent difference between exploitation and expropriation.

For Du Bois, this origin story created a second critical observation, that expropriation differs from exploitation not just economically, but also psychologically, through intense feelings of "inferiority . . . helplessness . . . and the submergence below the arbitrary will of any sort of individual."[24] Subsequently, we have the foundation for the narrative at the center of "The White Worker," who was not willing, after reaching America, to regard itself as a "permanent laboring class." This in essence is the initial spark of the kind of negative class consciousness examined in Parts 1 and 2, the result "a petty-bourgeoisie ready always to join capital in exploiting common labor, white and black, foreign and native."[25] No doubt today's designers have origins in such aspirations, unaware of the realities of their true economic and social positions, which theoretically should allow them to find solidarity with other workers, but instead creates workers who view themselves as always just a few steps away from the capital that suppresses them. For our contemporary building industry, Du Bois's observations around land are prescient, as the abundance of "free land" in America created an ideal of utopian emancipation through land, and hence building, rather than the traditional worker-based solidarity found in land-constrained Europe.[26] Here we have a discipline of architecture that is subsumed under the weight of larger American ideals; unaware of the origins of such a story, it only follows, and is in service to, those who create such ideology.

Du Bois's fourth chapter, "The General Strike," brings an important labor-centered understanding of the success of the Northern armies during the Civil War:

This was not merely a desire to stop work. It was a strike on a wide basis against the conditions of work. It was a general strike that involved directly in the end perhaps a half a million people. They wanted to stop the economy of the plantation system, and to do that they left the plantations.[27]

In other words, the withholding of labor through a large, general strike was one of the most powerful tools in dismantling the Southern power structure and uniting disparate factions of laborers. We can see the contemporary connection with Ni Una Menos, that when the most powerful elements of labor movements are united with the sharp critiques of a broad-based feminism, the deepest transformations to society are possible. In the case of Du Bois, these are certainly historical observations rooted directly in their context; however, one can begin to imagine an alternative in which the "White Worker" and the "Black Worker" maintained such a stance of solidarity through labor, with a simultaneous recognition of the differences of such labor. Fraser also considers race in a similar territory as gender, caught between the pull of movements of redistribution and recognition.[28] In this sense, this is the biggest tragedy of the Reconstruction era: the missed opportunity for a real form of cross-class *and* race solidarity that could have radically altered the course of the United States. A missed opportunity does not mean we must be limited by the failures of history, however. While labor has for too long been content to remain in its respective camps in terms of negotiations and strikes, a new generation of leaders like UAW president Shawn Fain has called for a general strike for not just his union, or all unions, but *all workers*, a radical charge that is reminiscent of Du Bois's observations.[29]

We can see these issues actually manifested in the development, or "un-development," of the United States in the aftermath of desegregation. Policy analyst and author Heather McGhee shares a revealing anecdote about the tendency for municipalities to damage their own environments rather than open their public spaces to African Americans per new legal standards. The town of Mobile, Alabama, for example, decided to fill its flourishing public pool with concrete rather than maintain it as a newly integrated space. McGhee considered this type of intentional self-inflicted harm "drained-pool politics," a kind of perverted zero-sum thinking in which advantages conferred to "Other" groups take away from advantages from those in power, in this case white people. McGhee translates this idea to a broader application of how racism, which views people of other races and ethnicities as competition toward achieving material success, is zero-sum thinking, instead imploring nonprofits, municipalities, community groups, and other organizations to understand that by supporting and helping the least among us we all flourish. In the former scenario we all suffer, but in the latter, we are all benefited.[30] Matrix understood this in their analysis of difficult urbanscapes filled with insurmountable stairs and blockading curbs. Similarly, labor movements like those of Gago that specifically target a broad coalition of races and ethnicities and design that seeks to tackle the most challenging problems in neglected neighborhoods are not only issues of "identity politics," or recognition, as Fraser would put it, but are examples of actions that are transformative as they benefit both the groups that need support the most and improve the quality of life for all.

ABOVE ALL, DESIGN IS IMPLICATED most strongly in our current environmental crises. With a history of prioritizing growth in order to sell its ideas and products, design has been at the center of many of the worst elements of human-led pollution, carbon emissions, and overall environmental degradation. The residential and commercial portion of the building sector is alone responsible for 30 percent of total emissions in the United States, not accounting for the myriad other sectors it intersects with.[31] Coupled with manufacturing computer parts, fast furniture, among many others, design is front and center in the climate crisis. And though it is easy to privilege action-oriented approaches to it, or critiques of capitalism, this should come with the honest admission that such approaches thus far have been inadequate, and the problem has become historic in nature.[32] As we have seen above, action, that is, praxis, is impoverished without theory, and though there has been a plethora of ecological theory, it has remained just that—*exclusively* ecological. Similarly, other disciplines have been equally content to give, at best, a performative nod to climate change, and at worst, continue as though they have no responsibility to provide solutions from their own perspective. For such a pressing problem, we need more than traditional theories and complacent disciplines content to remain within prescribed boundaries drawn from "rational" foundations of discrete, narrow definitions. Instead, we need ideas and movements that seek not just to "intersect" with one another, but learn and transform through a potent synthesis, taking the best of each and reshaping their forms of practice.

New propositions for unorthodox forms of synthesis between external disciplines and ecology must first begin with an understanding of the primary forms of knowledge privy to the latter. The two most common are Scientific Ecological Knowledge (SEK) and Traditional Ecological Knowledge (TEK). Summarized broadly, SEK privileges rationalization and a positive, conclusive (and aspirationally holistic) understanding of the environment. An essential form of this thinking is found in Descartes's *Rules for the Direction of the Mind*, in which the reader is immediately directed toward the goal of the text: "*The aim of our studies should be to direct the mind with a view to forming true and sound judgments about whatever comes before it.*"[33] In other words, the primary vantage point for forming any "true and sound judgment" must be made through the human mind, following a series of rational steps in which the reader can arrive at such logical conclusions.

Equally important to the modern-rational movement is Francis Bacon, who, along with Descartes, helped to initiate an age of learning outside of the confines of medieval scholasticism with its dependence on Aristotelian thinking. Unearthing the meandering history of "objectivity," historian Lorraine Daston places particular importance on Bacon and his insistence on utilizing "isolated facts" instead of a reliance on common experience and demonstrative universals.[34] In this sense, facts became synonymous with objectivity, as something existing outside of the "biased" view of relative experience among individuals or groups: "The familiar sense of the word 'fact' as 'a datum of experience, as distinguished from the conclusions that may be based on it' enters the English language contemporary with Bacon's writings in the early seventeenth century."[35] Experience is not necessarily eliminated per such a definition, but it is categorized through the notion of a neutral datum that rises above interpretation, as would have been the case in the use of universals found in Aristotelian thinking, for example.

This leads to the inevitable conclusion of empirical science not only presenting a truth, but *the* truth in relation to understanding the world around us. The implications of this conclusion would emerge rapidly, with European settlers moving through the "undiscovered world" with the tools necessary to understand, demarcate, divide, and reap from it. In his book *The Nutmeg's Curse*, writer Amitav Ghosh deftly articulates the "European projects" and their evolution through the conceptions of thinkers like Descartes and Bacon:

> It was the rendering of humans into mute resources that enabled the metaphysical leap whereby the Earth and everything in it could also be reduced to inertness.... Above all, it was the subjugation, and repopulating, of the Americas that enabled educated, upper-class European men to think of themselves as the subduers of everything they surveyed, even in their own countries, and especially within that domain they conceived of as "Nature"—an inert repository of resources, which, in order to be "improved," need to be expropriated, no matter whether from Amerindians or from English or Scottish peasants.[36]

Ghosh's work not only illuminates this important part of history, allowing us to more deeply understand the connections between race and the environment, but he draws important connections between it and our contemporary climate crisis, noting that it is only through this "metaphysical leap" that we can arrive at such a disastrous relationship with nature.

If SEK is dependent on rational articulations and objective enclosure, TEK presents an alternative conceptual model. Eschewing the positivism of SEK, TEK instead embraces learning not just about, but *with* nature, forgoing deterministic definitions and instead seeking integrated origins, stories, cycles, and relationships, with a humble acknowledgment that an all-encompassing understanding and demarcation of nature and its constituent elements is not only impossible but harmful to both nature and humans. One of the most prominent thinkers associated with TEK is Robin Wall Kimmerer, whose important text *Braiding Sweetgrass* introduced many to an idea the author was admittedly unfamiliar with herself. Early in her career, after having just received a PhD in Plant Ecology, Kimmerer recounts one of her meaningful encounters with Indigenous knowledge:

> A Navajo woman without a day of university botany training in her life ... spoke for hours and I hung on every word. One by one, name by name, she told of the plants in her valley. Where each one lived, when it bloomed, who it liked to live near and all its relationships, who ate it, who lined their nests with its fibers, what kind of medicine it offered.[37]

Though a member of the Citizen Potawatomi Nation, Kimmerer's education up until that point was completely subsumed by SEK. In this telling, natural elements such as plants are understood as characters, with their own perspective shared as part of their own individual story and its connection to others, all moving through a relational cycle. This is in contrast to Descartes, whose rules sought to isolate things observed through the human mind as individual instances, forming links in a chain to comprehensive knowledge of the matter at hand.[38] Though comparatively rigid, Descartes's methods helped generations of scientists and thinkers develop prolific advances in mathematics, physics, and medicine, areas to which Descartes himself contributed greatly, setting the stage for the Enlightenment and subsequent progress in the Western world.

However, because it must operate in such limited constraints, SEK misses those elements that cannot be neatly categorized. Ghosh shares such ineffable ways of knowing among the Bandanese, the characters at the heart of his book, and their differing, "hidden" understanding of the nutmeg central to the power struggle of Dutch settlers.[39] This mystery, however, can be seen as both the greatest strength and weakness of TEK, as the inability to explicate knowledge is simultaneously mesmerizing and obfuscating, an ontology that can prove inaccessible for those on the outside of its teachings.

What we might label Design Knowledge (DK), on the other hand, is less concerned with an oppositional force, such as the schism between TEK and SEK, and instead is interested in everything conceived of by humans. While the term "design" is nebulous, touching nearly every aspect of the human condition, it can best be understood through *what it does* rather than a conceptual or analytical definition. Design historians Hazel Clark and David Brody provide a comprehensive list of the things design "does": "It improves and gives direction to our lives ... creates new possibilities in our physical world that are not based in nature ... [it] is about assistance, but it can also be a hindrance ... [it] uses experiences from the past to create things for the present that look forward to the future." In other words, "Design is everywhere."[40] Necessarily broad, this definition gives design the benefit of intersecting with nearly every arena of human life, from the creation of new lifesaving medical equipment to every bit of technological interface, to the most intimate physical surroundings of our homes. However, it is also problematic for the same reason, as it is so vast that it can claim a sort of transcendence above, or ignorance to, other issues, particularly environmental and social struggles. Privileging problem-solving through technical expertise, design knowledge, according to this definition, is embedded with an aloof agnosticism. Ignoring those problems that are concerned with the messy struggles in the social realm, via Gago and Du Bois, Design Knowledge has instead remained too preoccupied with the complexity of its own niche interests, designing for luxury and creating self-serving exhibitions, for example. Though technically impressive, all of this has come at the expense of the concerns of everyday life.

In order to begin to repair the schism between TEK and SEK with the help of DK, we can look to a historical analysis through which a useful concept emerges, that of the notion of the "metabolic rift" found in Marx's writing on the agricultural developments of his time. Sociologist John Bellamy Foster, in his paper "Marx's Theory of Metabolic Rift: Classical Foundations for Environmental Sociology," provided some of the first analysis that sought to bring a strong ecological element to Marx's thinking. Importantly, Foster incorporates a fundamental aspect of Marx's theorizing, that of privileging "social relations" in understanding areas such as economics and politics. Foster centers his analysis on the divide between "town and country" and the crisis of depleting nutritional value of soil:

> Moreover, this could be seen as related not only to the soil but to the antagonism between town and country. For Marx, like Liebig, the failure to recycle nutrients to the soil had its counterpart in the pollution of the cities and the irrationality of modern sewage systems. In Capital (Volume 3), he observed: "In London . . . they can do nothing better with the excrement produced by 4 1/2 million people than pollute the Thames with it, at monstrous expense."[41]

Here is the first identification that social relations, in the form of a rift between those living in the city and those living in the country, produced a disruption in the quality of the soil. While residents of the city were utilizing the crops grown in the country, the cycle of nutrients returning to the soil through urban human and animal excrement was broken by the harshness of the urban environment in the form of a metabolic rift.[42] In turn, this physical barrier was also predicated on the physical gap between things, as those in the city were alienated from the production of their food sources, and those producing the food were alienated from those who consumed it. In other words, though it is not explicitly stated, this particular *social* rift is also a *spatial* one in the sense that it is both the productive and physical distance between two groups of people that are responsible for the problem at hand.

A contemporary example useful for underscoring the importance of the metabolic rift is the evidence of soil disruption in the aftermath of Hurricane Katrina. This storm devastated New Orleans, a city infrastructurally opposed to its local ecology, and one that perilously neglected the natural rhythms of the Mississippi River. Unlike much of the United States, the Louisiana Delta is an alluvial landscape, meaning its soil is dependent on regular flooding to deposit sediment, replenishing the relatively young geological landscape. As urban infrastructure developed and machinery like cars became a regular part of city life, the regular flooding of the Mississippi proved undesirable. Additionally, the discovery of rich oil deposits in the region, necessary for the production of so many of our designed goods today, accelerated the need for hard engineering solutions like canals and levees to keep the rhythms of nature at bay.[43] While the failure of the Army Corps of Engineers to adequately design these levees is the most infamous contributor to the calamity, less known is the role of the battle between "town" and "nature," in this case, river. Evidence of this neglect can be found in the proliferation of construction of "slab-on-grade" homes (the concrete foundation sits directly on top of the ground) during the post–Second World War boom in lieu of structures raised on piers, as is the case for historic homes that are elevated to account for the regular rhythms of water. Through my service as an AmeriCorps member and as part of the city's rebuilding effort, we would regularly provide tours for our volunteers of the neighborhoods most impacted. In these neighborhoods, often developed through such environmentally ignorant building methods, the destructive qualities of both the storm and the "metabolic rift" were on full display. The Lower Ninth Ward, a predominantly Black neighborhood pushed to the margins of the city in one of the geographically lowest areas and not coincidentally most obliterated by the failure of its infrastructure,[44] also houses an observation deck overlooking

Bayou Bienvenue. This once critical artery in the historic city, along with the Mississippi River, provided ideal passage for non-fossil-fueled ships, utilizing the discrete passage from the Gulf of Mexico into the city where ships would be dismantled and rebuilt in the form of simple homes and furniture. This is where the term "barge board" comes from and is why so many historic homes in New Orleans are made of it. Though the lumber was harvested, this reuse of materials for multiple purposes that extend the life cycle of the material (and the time for the regrowth of trees) provides a design-based counter-example to the metabolic rift. Today, however, the evidence of the rift is stark; one can face toward the water and see the remnants of cypress stumps that have died as a result of saltwater intrusion from the oil-moving canals. Behind them are the remnants of homes in the forms of concrete stoops, the only elements left standing. For our volunteers, especially from places in the northeast like New York and New Jersey, although distressing, this remained a local problem. That sense of compartmentalized safety was shattered, however, when Hurricane Sandy wreaked havoc on their own homes, the problem shifting from specific to universal. As philosopher Olúfẹ́mi O. Táíwò says in his call for climate justice, "Everywhere is New Orleans." It is only a matter of time that all of us will face such realities.[45]

The land and its direct inhabitants are not the only victims of the metabolic rift. Ecofeminist Vandana Shiva also leverages components of Marx's critique in order to address the gaps in conventional ecological thinking, in this case through the metaphor of the lifeboat on the *Titanic*. While many see heroic actions in allowing women and children to proceed first in the event of crisis, and rightfully so, Shiva is quick to point out that there is an important qualification to this scenario, that those women and children are primarily affluent. Extending this metaphor into conventional notions of development around the world, Shiva critiques the narrow scope of such "progressive" forces, those that both SEK and DK happily leverage in order to take advantage of potent market forces. Here, because of the "ideology of development," certain groups and practices are dismissed as impoverished while those that blindly follow the vicissitudes of the market are rewarded:

> Culturally perceived poverty is not necessarily real material poverty: subsistence economies that satisfy basic needs through self-provisioning are not poor in the sense of deprivation. Yet the ideology of development declares them to be so because they neither participate overwhelmingly in the market economy nor consume commodities produced for and distributed through the market, even though they might be satisfying those basic needs through self-provisioning mechanisms.[46]

Specifically mentioning housing and design-based production, Shiva continues, not only invalidating the ideology of development, but underscoring the real benefits that "anti-development" forms of being bring to communities:

> On the contrary, millets, for example, are nutritionally superior to processed foods, houses built with local materials rather than concrete are better adapted to the local climate and ecology, natural fibers are generally preferable to synthetic ones—and often more affordable. The cultural perception of prudent subsistence living as poverty has provided legitimization for the development process as a "poverty-removal" project. "Development" as a culturally biased process destroys wholesome and sustainable lifestyles and instead creates real material poverty, or misery, by denying the means of survival through the diversion of resources to resource-intensive commodity production.[47]

This observation is a real challenge to design in general. How do we square the dependence on industrialized production and consumption, which propels so much of the design industry, with the reality that less development would be better for the environment? Shiva's insight to local building and production processes holds key concepts that, while difficult to translate to urban development in the United States, can form important ethical principles for future development, especially in the age of climate crisis.

Social critic and educator bell hooks also recognized that the rift between town and country is fundamental to understanding the ecological crisis. Describing her upbringing in the foothills of Kentucky, hooks reflected on the sanctuary that such an environment provided for her childhood. For hooks it transcended many of the manmade sociological categories that are baked into urban life: "Before is the isolated life we lived as a family in the Kentucky hills, a life where the demarcations of race, class, and gender did not matter. What mattered was the line separating country and city—nature mattered."[48] This is a very important critique of urbanity on two levels: first, that the cacophony and isolation of life in the city is easily ameliorated by the sanctuary of nature, and two, that the city is built on divisions beyond just physical ones, but also on the fundamental schisms of race, class, and gender. It is also a clever subversion of the stereotype of the "White country" and "Black city," emphasizing the history of Black displacement during the Great Migration, with families uprooted from their "agrarian past," leaving behind "cultures of belonging" that had been built over generations.[49] For hooks, this agrarian past is both a distant and immediate one, as her family and most true expressions of self, and hence the Black experience, are most strongly felt in the country. In contrast, the city, with its disruption of community ties and erasure of agrarian history, begins to stifle such freedom with its insistence on systematic separations.

This rift manifests itself from the larger social and psychological scales evidenced by the critics above to the scale of individual buildings. Though the agrarian manifestation of the rift in Marx's time is still with us today, increasingly complex technology found within building systems has created a more acute rift between the inhabitants of buildings and the metabolism of buildings, or the energy necessary to run the interconnected array of technology and systems required of a twenty-first-century building. Prior to the advent of contemporary building systems, the most common form of heat production, for example, was that of combustion via wood or coal, just like hooks's family home used in Kentucky. Though we now know this produces the least desirable form of carbon emissions, there *is* an intimacy with the process of production; the wood must come from somewhere, and even if not *sourced* directly, it must be *placed* directly in the fireplace by the person who needs warmth. This was also true of the densest urban environments, countless chimneys dotting the horizon line, each household directly responsible for at least a significant portion of the process of heating their homes.

A major technological revolution occurred during the twentieth century: shifting from decentralized direct combustion forms of heating, buildings began to utilize centralized systems, with equipment like boilers, supplied by gas or oil, generating heat that was then distributed through various rooms in individual homes, or units within larger buildings, most commonly through steam radiators. These same systems were used at the site of mass production, as factories required large furnaces, shop floors, and offices that integrated more and more complex strategies for a controlled climate. Today, this same centralized approach is nearly universal in both town and country, with other systems utilizing electricity or conditioned air. Whether combustion, electrical, or conditioned air, all of these contemporary systems have one thing in common: though spatially efficient, they preclude the inhabitants from understanding the full "metabolism" of the building's energy production, comfortable ambient temperatures magically arriving with the flip of a switch, or as in the case in many large cities in the United States, no involvement by the inhabitants at all. In this sense, this form of energy appears as a "free gift of nature."

While all these authors and perspectives offer vital critiques of our relationship to town and country, they are all inherently dependent on the strict dichotomy between the two, not unlike the rift between SEK and TEK. As such, it is too easy to read such critiques with a strong anti-urban lens, with the city a place of corruption of the purity of nature. For Marx, the voracious city robs the soil of its key nutrients; for Shiva, development occurs at the detriment of too many; and for hooks, New York City becomes a place of isolation and identity-based constriction in opposition to the unbounded hills of Kentucky.[50] This is not to say that any of these views are invalid, but to underscore that they are dependent on a largely *negative* view of the city and *positive* view of nature. Useful on a certain ethical level, helping us keep an eye toward natural places and beings uncorrupted by the trappings of human machinations (and reminding us of our long history and where we come from), this kind of dichotomy breaks down quickly when examining contemporary data regarding place-based emission sources. While in the United States cities like Los Angeles and New York are regarded as the epitome of industrialized waste, automobile pollution, and overall environmental destruction, because of their density relative to the suburban sprawl and rural enclaves surrounding them, large cities and the states they are located in have lower carbon emissions per capita, complicating the notion of which areas are more harmful to the environment.[51] hooks too hints at the problematic dependency on the rift, both lamenting the strip mining common in her native Kentucky while simultaneously acknowledging that "Coal is one of earth's great gifts,"[52] keeping her family and its protective embrace warm on cold nights.

Returning to Foster, who not only unearthed a strong ecological theory from Marx via the concept of metabolic rift, but also offered an important bit of reflection on the relationship between his discipline, sociology, and ecology, we can begin to understand the importance of the critique of these dichotomies:

> Ironically, the chief problem with this contrast between the human exemptionalist paradigm and the new environmental paradigm is that, even while emphasizing environmental factors, it tended to perpetuate a dualistic view of society versus the physical environment, anthropocentrism versus ecocentrism, and thus easily fell into the fallacy of the excluded middle (or a false dichotomy). There is a tendency in this view to see any theory that emphasizes

socioeconomic progress or cultural accumulation as thereby "anthropocentric" and opposed to an "ecocentric" perspective, which seeks to decenter the human world and human interests. Nevertheless, logic suggests that there is no reason for such a stark opposition, since there are numerous ways in which sociology can embrace a concern for ecological sustainability without abandoning its emphasis on the development of human culture and production.[53]

Foster spells out exactly what a "synthesis," or dialectic, of disciplines would look like. For Foster, Marx's foresight to see the agricultural problems of his day through the connection between town and country was an early significant accomplishment of sociology. Further, it is a concrete example of how sociology can move beyond its disciplinarian boundaries through the intense study of ecological issues, and that "ecological analysis, devoid of sociological insight, is incapable of dealing with the contemporary crisis of the earth—a crisis which has its source and its meaning ultimately in society itself."[54]

Here, Foster's call should extend to *all* disciplines, for we are in a moment of not just localized ecological crises, but a literal planetary-scale crisis that requires all hands on deck, so to speak. Following this, we can consider that which is "designed" synonymous with "anthropocentric," for what is more human-centered than the making of our built environment and products through our own labor? Ecology too is in need of a partnership with design, with its ability to analyze complex, abstract problems and propose concrete, material solutions. This would require a deep reconception of each. On the one hand, design must be willing to take ownership of its tendency to privilege an ideology that encourages conspicuous, unnecessary consumption in the pursuit of trends and profit, while on the other, ecology must open its closed scientific borders, which views other disciplines as incompetent or ignorant of the serious analysis only it is privy to. Specifically, ecology must recognize that the road to environmental redemption runs through the city, not around or above it. In other words, both design and ecology can be liberated from their restrictive discipline-based boundaries in order to learn from each other and thus become more effective in the problems they each typically address.

It is not difficult to see the connection between Foster's "false dichotomy" and the contentious relationship between SEK and TEK. Though Kimmerer provides us with a strong definition of TEK, her work also demonstrates an example of a move toward synthesis with SEK, asking questions about beauty, for example, in a discipline that is quick to explain such concepts as chemical reactions or instinctual devices. Kimmerer's instincts to trust the stories that the natural world is telling compel her to ask unorthodox questions "because science as a way of knowing is too narrow for the task."[55] This could be said of many forms of knowledge and production; in the case of design, a narrow focus on solving problems as efficiently as possible through ever-increasingly technical means, with a disregard for the implications of privileging such deterministic values, that is, the progression from the intimate production of energy to the alienated systems hidden within our walls. Considered together, both Kimmerer and Foster give us a working definition for a kind of knowledge that does not rely on the false dichotomy between SEK and TEK, or ecology and other disciplines, but rather begins to not just borrow, but *synthesize* important aspects of each. From science, a rigorous empiricism that is dependent on the observation of real facts, not assumptions or faith. From "tradition," a sense of wonder and an enchantment of the natural world, and along with it, a refusal to draw premature boundaries of "knowing."

While theoretical synthesis is key to addressing the "false dichotomy," we are in a moment that requires material examples of solutions to the conceptual fracture, and also the physical ills of our planet. The built environment is at the center of this critical conversation: how can a synthesis between SEK and TEK help us combat the problems that have led to the rift between town and country? Many on the left balk at the notion of technical solutions in regard to the climate crisis; however, as Andreas Malm argues, some combination of mitigation, management, and removal of carbon dioxide is necessary, an uncomfortably nuanced position from someone well acquainted with the real scope of the problem.[56] Marx also was not opposed to technology; conversely, he was a proponent of technological development, but most critical of the relations between who uses them and who develops them.[57] Ghosh, too, is willing to view the built environment and its technological solutions as an integral part of combating a changing climate:

> Energy derived from sources like the sun, air, and water, on the other hand, is imbued with immense liberatory potential. In principle every house, farm, and factory could free itself from the grid by generating its own power. No longer would long power lines and gigantic, leak-prone tankers be needed for the transportation of energy, no longer would workers have to toil in underground mines or in remote deserts and rough seas; there would be no need for the long supply chains required by fossil fuels.[58]

These technical solutions not only provide means for mitigating the release of carbon into the atmosphere, they also address the ecological rift manifested in the spatial relation of our alienation from power sources in buildings. In a project I worked on in the Rockaways, Queens, we used several methods of energy production that do just this. Rather than typical heating sources heavily dependent on carbon, we leveraged the earth's energy through a closed-loop geothermal system, a form of engineering that, harnessing massive amounts of "free" energy, cycles the constant temperature of the earth to heat the building in the winter and sink excess heat while cooling in the summer. This process can even extend beyond a single building through a form of energy sharing, a deeply renewable process that has huge potential for urban areas. Through solar panels, the essentially boundless energy from the sun is harvested in the form of electricity produced immediately on-site, not in a power plant intentionally placed in disadvantaged communities.

Each day, residents of this building will be able to look outside and see the direct relationship between the sun and their lamps, a not so small act against alienation. And through design principles that are familiar to Pueblo Indians of the American Southwest, for example, the building adheres to Passive House standards, using thicker wall assemblies and copious amounts of insulation and air sealing in order to effectively store the heating and cooling created, vastly reducing the overall demand of the building.

All of these sources intertwine to create a site in which nearly all of the energy is produced in immediate proximity to those who live there. This is not unlike the generation of electricity through solar panels for EV charging at residences, underscoring the importance of labor's win in claiming responsibility for the manufacturing of EV batteries, a concrete example of the kind of synthesis between social movements we are searching for.[59] Though not as immediately visible as the wood-burning fireplace, these forms of energy creation are just as spatially close, and far less destructive toward the environment. The solar panels are certainly visible, eliminating the need for natural gas in apartment units. The Passive House design standards and geothermal energy strategies may not be directly visible, but they might be felt through lower energy bills and more comfortable interior environments. And residents will definitively know that their home has been designed to the highest energy efficiency standards. Beyond the scale of individual buildings, elements of design are beginning to reorient themselves from rationalized measurements of productiveness and monetary value toward valuing "unproductive" animal life, as is the case of a new wilderness bridge in Los Angeles, a project that creates a vital link for the population of mountain lions in the area.[60] In a city whose identity is completely dominated by cars, this is the sort of example in which urban environments can begin to shift their own consciousness and adopt the values of ecology while leaning on the sophisticated designs of engineers and landscape architects.

None of this amounts to a holistic solution to the climate crisis; we are far beyond a single solution at such a magnitude. However, such technical fixes are impactful because they address the schism between our conceptual understanding of the environment and our material engagement with it.

Though our designed urban environments do considerable harm to the environment, they are also necessary for the implementation of our best solutions. Rather than viewing such spaces as the exclusive domain of purely rational, "objective" planning, perhaps they can be understood as integral components in the reduction of carbon emissions through density and mitigation, doing more than the rural and suburban areas supposedly more in tune with nature via a closer proximity to it. The increased presence of whales and dolphins in a cleaner East River and other bodies of water surrounding New York City speaks to our potential to live a more intertwined existence, much like wildlife bridges, enriching and expanding our experience of the natural world around us.[61] Materially, our designed urban environments might also continue to engender their own metabolic cycles, reducing dependence on distant forms of production and instead maintaining their own local metabolisms at the scale of the block, building, and even apartment. Our cities are here to stay, and they are far too important to dismiss as part of our surrounding ecology; without them, we miss a chance to not only better the planet, but enrich our everyday lives, reshaping the very values that might finally repair our broken relationship with the environment.

CONCLUSION

What Is the Architecture of Labor?

It is the province of art to set the true ideal of a full and reasonable life before him, a life to which the perception and creation of beauty, the enjoyment of real pleasure that is, shall be felt to be as necessary to man as his daily bread, and that no man, and no set of men, can be deprived of this except by mere opposition, which should be resisted to the utmost.
—WILLIAM MORRIS, *HOW I BECAME A SOCIALIST*

As an ultimate goal, it is crucial to synthesize all of the disparate movements discussed in this book and use them as a framework that has radical potential.[1] Otherwise, we will remain in isolated encampments, which might achieve decent, but not broadly meaningful wins. Further, we have to begin to shift our hope from corporatized political parties, which serve the interests of the few, and instead pivot our desire for change within groups with broad interests and the improvement of material conditions for the many. In this way, in order to look forward, we should begin by centering our coalesced movement within the urban, the localized environment in which not only our individual and small group lives overlap, but where they have the best potential to unite in a potent form of solidarity.

Geographer David Harvey's work in reinvigorating the concept of the "right to the city," first articulated by philosopher Henri Lefebvre, holds the strongest potential for threading together elements that might appear unrelated, or stubbornly resist integration with "outsiders." Writing in *Rebel Cities*, Harvey repeatedly draws attention to "cultural production" as a crucial component of the production of cities, recognizing those who *actually* make the city, unlike the developers and other members of the ruling class who primarily control the financing and other market transactions behind the real production. He observes:

> The number of workers engaged in cultural activities and production has increased considerably over the past few decades (from some 150,000 registered in the New York metropolitan region in the 1980s to likely more than double that by now), and continues to rise. They form the creative core of what Daniel Bell calls "the cultural mass". . . and have shifted in their political stances over the years. In the 1960s, the art colleges were hotbeds of radical discussion, but their subsequent pacification and professionalization has seriously diminished agitational politics. Though socialist strategy and thought may need to be reconfigured, revitalizing such institutions as centers of political engagement and mobilizing the political and agitational powers of cultural producers is surely a worthwhile objective for the left.[2]

It is certainly the case that cultural production has lost much of its radical tendencies since the 1960s, instead pairing increasing specialization and professionalization with the seductive forces of the market. However, the emerging work of organizing design labor, the analysis in this book, and other various cultural movements that center their aims in labor and societal change, certainly fall into Harvey's categorization. More than a decade after the publication of *Rebel Cities*, there has been an upsurge in the mobilization he called for, with unionization in particular growing in these sectors in ways

CONCLUSION

not seen in many decades. While this work is just beginning, it is safe to say that a fire has been kindled.

However, we must, on the one hand, maintain this young movement, and on the other, do the difficult and complicated work of envisioning it beyond unionization alone. Harvey writes:

> But popular culture as produced through the common relationships of daily life is also crucial. Here lies one of the key spaces of hope for the construction of an alternative kind of globalization and a vibrant anti-commodification politics: one in which the progressive forces of cultural production and transformation can seek to appropriate and undermine the forces of capital rather than the other way around.[3]

Up until this point, it has certainly been "the other way around" with design. The "unique" class consciousness of design disciplines has had, as we have seen, important implications for the origin of their individualized sense of identity, but also specific form of exploitation. And these forces are still compelling today. With increased economic precariousness comes a counter-balancing effort to distinguish and differentiate, through the means explored above. As many design disciplines feel the threat of specialization, automation, and other increasingly dominant forces of our time, they risk continuing to succumb to a false consciousness that feels real, but one that pushes them into potential irrelevance. This can create a dangerous downward spiral that negates these potential agents of change, both economically and from a class perspective, alienating them from not only the money, but other social groups and classes. This makes it necessary to temporarily suspend such deeply entrenched ways of being through a broader understanding of class when engaging with issues of labor, specifically in its relation to other classes. We must take the advice of Karl Polanyi, who calls us to identify with "interests wider than [our] own."[4]

Historian E. P. Thompson's work is also encouraging for designers for our forward-looking gaze, as his historical work shows that the unique literary and cultural production of artisans, in the form of self-taught radical intellectualism, paved the way for broader social change.[5] In today's labor movement, we see a potential parallel from unionized workers at companies like Condé Nast, responsible for such cultural publications as *The New Yorker, Vanity Fair, Pitchfork,* and *Architectural Digest*. The infrastructure for such "radical intellectualism" is already in place, and with it we shouldn't be intimidated by a lack of formal education in politics, or an unfamiliarity with organizing. We can point to those successful nineteenth-century artisan movements, which relied heavily on self-education. This allows us to eschew both the overly cumbersome and increasingly irrelevant studio education of designers, as well as the myopic definition provided by professional practice. Though the past movements analyzed by Thompson occurred during the painful transition from the practice of artisans and craft guilds to mass production and industrialization, hence limiting efficacy in some ways,[6] our current historical moment is very different, one in which we find the entrenched shackles of credentialism and specialization suffocating our ability to think critically and independently. If we admit that craft within our disciplines, at least in the traditional sense, died long ago, and with it the pluralistic opportunity for a comfortable petty-bourgeois existence, our own historical moment presents a potentially more radical opportunity for change.

Paired with the work of deconstructing our false class consciousness, and building a new one, we should also embody the radicalism of Thompson's craftsmen in the work of imagining a new society *through* our unionization efforts, with our long-term goals broader than simply strong design unions, but rather a more just society. Historically, labor unions were their most successful when embracing a radical-social tradition, according to economist and labor historian Michael Yates. Leading with the ability for pragmatic yet progressive thinking, the original members of the CIO (Congress of Industrial Organizations) were not content to settle for better wages alone, but also fought for a society "where workers had rights and some control over their lives; where they were more than factors

CONCLUSION

of production. In this vision, people stuck together as a matter of principle, irrespective of their gender or race."[7] As Yates interprets this period, unions were not an end but a mechanism for achieving broad policies that benefit all workers, such as "full employment, progressive taxes, an end to militarism and empire, support for public investment in health, education, and welfare, and solidarity with workers around the world."[8] One could imagine the growing unionization effort in publishing, through the likes of Condé Nast Union, which represents a large umbrella of cultural magazines, taking up the literary radicalism via Thompson by directly supporting traditional labor with style. Artists in these circles and elsewhere could be called to shift their attention (and money) away from the interests of the ruling class and toward support for the work described by Yates through an "art for the millions."[9] Or perhaps, following the calls for climate justice from the philosopher Táíwò, unions might share their knowledge of collective bargaining, collaborating with "community organizations to bargain with corporations over a wider set of demands that benefit the entire communities that workers come from and represent, that is, for the common good."[10] If we as designers engender such a radical ethos within the aims of our discipline, we also might be viewed as an integral part of a mass movement centered on the many and not the few.

Beyond the urban, one could imagine a revitalization of large-scale projects such as the Tennessee Valley Authority, a centralized government agency that can synthesize workers and social interests. Although similar agencies existed at one time or another across the country,[11] the TVA is a more comprehensive precedent for many reasons, with three of primary importance: first, the scale of impact and coordination possible through its now rare type of organization; second, the collective nature of the work; and third, the wide range of scales the agency worked through. Responding to the ecological crisis of deforestation (a "rift" at the hands of over-farming) and a lack of public services, primarily electricity, its establishment as a government agency allowed it to forgo the bidding processes known to slow down and increase the cost of large projects in the United

States,[12] not only building large works like dams and bridges, but restoring the landscape through reforestation and the introduction of modern farming techniques in lieu of the methods of the past, which favored the clearing and abandoning of land. Perhaps most interesting, its architects, working in the TVA's Architect's Office, are little known by name today, as cooperation and collective thinking were the values that drove the design process, not individual notoriety. Roland A. Wank, scarcely mentioned in architectural history courses, embodied this socially forward thinking, pushing the TVA to design projects beyond its large infrastructure portfolio including public parks, meeting halls, and cooperative housing.[13] Design was not limited to the scale of infrastructure; perhaps most surprisingly, there was even a Ceramics Research Laboratory, a quixotic leg of the overall project to bring utilitarian consumer goods like cookware and appliances to a region lacking electricity and basic, affordable household equipment.[14] While these "modest" attributes are unheard of in today's design circles, they were part and parcel of one of the most impactful government programs in U.S. history; for these designers, their solidaristic aspirations were both personal and public, intended to serve as many as possible, a reciprocal relation of collectivity over individuality.

Although there is much valid critique about the negligence of the TVA, particularly its connection to the war economy via the Manhattan Project, and the WPA in general, especially toward communities that had little say in the direction of projects that would dramatically transform their homes and backyards, we should not accept the failures of the past as destined to repeat themselves. It is inarguable that much harm was caused, but many of the most transformative and long-lasting infrastructure projects in the United States came out of this era, and we have collectively struggled to address any issue at scale since the dissolution of it. As we face numerous unprecedented crises that are vastly complex and intertwined, we are in desperate need of centralized agencies that can collectively leverage both the skills of professionals like the TVA did, while at the same time incorporating the progress we have

CONCLUSION

made through social movements since the 1960s. Alternatively, local governments at the scale of the city can reflect on the success of municipal movements like "Sewer Socialism" found in Milwaukee in the early twentieth century, building agencies that simultaneously fight corruption while foregrounding a strategy of "back-to-basics" through the development of functioning transit systems and healthy parks.[15]

Too often there is opposition in the United States, from both sides of the political aisle, toward government endeavors such as the TVA or public housing, an understandable but shortsighted response to years of cultivated mistrust. This ideological project, catalyzing during the Reagan presidency, has entrenched market-based, individualistic thinking through all aspects of society; it is no surprise that one of Reagan's crowning achievements was the firing of striking air traffic controllers. However, as the strength of this paradigm wanes, we have an opportunity to reimagine old political projects. Rather than an overly bureaucratic agency, a reimagined TVA in every state could combine the strengths of centralized state organization with a form of real participatory democracy, with ordinary citizens contributing their voices to the direction of the projects chosen, for example. Similarly, city councils centered on the practical needs of their constituents can once again prove that public service is just that. If such reimagined agencies for our collective future were built on massive government investment through a progressive tax system, skilled trade union labor and a robust service corps, along with the holistic social values in the vein of Du Bois and others, we might stand a chance to save not only our severed social bonds but also our environment at large.

Embracing such radical notions allows us to ask equally radical questions: If we as a society valued craft, or safety, or quality more, should not developers be working for us? Wouldn't the developers then be at the service of the actual things being made instead of finance and profit? What would tech companies look like if they heeded the caution and knowledge of their union members over that of zealous founders? This kind of backwards thinking that marketization produces is the reason such questions sound radical. Through a reimagined unionization effort, however, we might begin to build a movement that can challenge the authority of capital, with quality of life once again our chief concern.

Many design schools and emerging professionals are deeply worried about the relationship between their disciplines and the "polycrisis" of our time.[16] As we confront the reality of multiple intertwined crises ranging from pandemic to financial collapse to environmental degradation, we need movements that work through equally expansive "polysolutions." Though academic studios might interrogate interesting questions around a lack of affordable housing, for example, or the ways in which design supports colonialism or racist regimes, the reality is that such efforts are nothing more than lip service without theoretical research beyond the confines of pseudo-intellectual design writing and real material action. For the former, we must reach beyond entrenched discourses of design, which have a limited audience. For the latter, unions offer such an integral starting point. But organizing is difficult, and it is easier to design a theoretical project or write a loosely researched critique than to do the slow work of building deep relationships and confronting power structures through pragmatic means. Even more difficult is creating organizations that do not only operate as social support clubs, or advocacy groups for issues through the one-way perspective of how design is impacted. Design must instead further itself by engaging both fronts, leaving behind the comforts of its deeply entrenched ways of knowing by reaching into unfamiliar territory.

In other words, is there an ability for architecture and design professionals to integrate both a visionary *and* political consciousness via their unique perspectives in both the artistic and the practical? While most of this book provides a missing analysis of how we got to our current state, we are also in desperate need of every sector and discipline to reimagine its role in the twenty-first century. As such, it is also a call for designers to be much more than they have been traditionally, to not passively adopt the short-sighted needs

CONCLUSION

of capital, the shallow calls of developers and business interests, the destructive demands of consumerism and commodification, or simply lament such forces through shallow critiques. It is a call to reignite the great humanist tradition historically associated with those who have not just dutifully, but joyfully, and most important, optimistically envisioned not only what the world is lacking but what it might become. If this isn't design, then what is it?

SELECTED BIBLIOGRAPHY

Berggren, Christian. *Alternatives to Lean Production: Work Organization in the Swedish Auto Industry*. 1992. Reprint, Ithaca, NY: Cornell University Press, 2019.

Braverman, Harry. *Labor and Monopoly Capital: The Degradation of Work in the Twentieth Century*. New York: Monthly Review Press, 1974.

Clark, Hazel, and David Brody. *Design Studies: A Reader*. 2009. Reprint, UK: Bloomsbury Academic, 2016.

Du Bois, W. E. B., *Black Reconstruction in America*. 1935. Reprint, New York: The Free Press, 1998.

Foster, John Bellamy. "Marx's Theory of Metabolic Rift: Classical Foundations for Environmental Sociology." *American Journal of Sociology* 105/2 (September 1999): 366–405.

Franklin, Samuel W. *The Cult of Creativity: A Surprising History*. Chicago: University of Chicago Press, 2023.

Fraser, Nancy. "A Triple Movement? Parsing the Politics of Crisis after Polanyi." *New Left Review* 81 (May 2013): 119–32.

Fraser, Nancy. "From Redistribution to Recognition? Dilemmas of Justice in a 'Post-Socialist' Age." *New Left Review* 212 (July 1995): 68–93.

Fraser, Nancy. *The Old Is Dying and the New Cannot Be Born*. London, New York: Verso Books, 2019.

Freire, Paulo, and Myra Bergman Ramos. *Pedagogy of the Oppressed*. London: Penguin Books, 1985.

Gago, Verónica, and Liz Mason-Deese. *Feminist International: How to Change Everything*. London; New York: Verso, 2020.

Ghosh, Amitav. *The Nutmeg's Curse: Parables for a Planet in Crisis*. Chicago: University of Chicago Press, 2022.

Harvey, David. *Rebel Cities: From the Right to the City to the Urban Revolution*. 2012. Reprint, Brooklyn, NY: Verso, 2019.

hooks, bell. *Belonging: A Culture of Place*. New York: Routledge, 2009.

Kimmerer, Robin Wall. *Braiding Sweetgrass: Indigenous Wisdom, Scientific Knowledge and the Teachings of Plants*. Minneapolis: Milkweed Editions, 2013.

Lefebvre, Henri, and John Moore. *Critique of Everyday Life: The One-Volume Edition*. London; New York: Verso, 2014.

Lukács, Georg. *History and Class Consciousness*. Cambridge, MA: The MIT Press, 1968.

Culvahouse, Tim, ed. *The Tennessee Valley Authority: Design and Persuasion*. New York: Princeton Architectural Press, 2007.

Malm, Andreas. "Planning the Planet." In *Has It Come to This?: The Promises and Perils of Geoengineering on the Brink*, edited by J. P. Sapinski, Holly Jean Buck, and Andreas Malm. New Brunswick, NJ: Rutgers University Press, 2020.

Marx, Karl, and Friedrich Engels. *The Communist Manifesto*, London: Penguin, 2002.

Marx, Karl, translated by Ben Fowkes. *Capital: A Critique of Political Economy*, vol. 1. Harmondsworth, UK: Penguin in association with *New Left Review*, 1990.

Matrix. *Making Space: Women and the Man-Made Environment*. London: Pluto Press, 1985.

McAlevey, Jane. *A Collective Bargain: Unions, Organizing, and the Fight for Democracy*. New York: HarperCollins, 2020.

McGhee, Heather C. *The Sum of Us: What Racism Costs Everyone and How We Can Prosper Together*. New York: One World, 2021.

Mills, C. Wright. *White Collar: The American Middle Classes*. 1951. Reprint, New York, NY: Oxford University Press, 2002.

Morris, William. *Useful Work v. Useless Toil*. London and New York: Penguin Books, 2008.

Polanyi, Karl. *The Great Transformation: The Political and Economic Origins of Our Time*. 1944. Reprint, Boston: Beacon Press, 2001.

Sennett, Richard, and Jonathan Cobb. *The Hidden Injuries of Class*. 1972. Reprint, New York: Norton, 1993.

Stone, Harris. *Workbook of an Unsuccessful Architect*. New York: Monthly Review Press, 1974.

Tafuri, Manfredo. *Architecture and Utopia: Design and Capitalist Develop-

ment. Translated by Barbara Luigia La Penta. Cambridge, MA: MIT Press, 1976.
Thompson, E. P., and Dorothy Thompson. *The Essential E. P. Thompson*. New York: Free Press, 2001.
Walker, John A., and Judy Attfield. *Design History and History of Design*. 1989. Reprint, London: Pluto, 1994.
Weber, Max, Hans Heinrich Gerth, Charles Wright Mills, and Bryan S. Turner. *From Max Weber: Essays in Sociology*. New York: Routledge, 2009.
Woods, Mary N. *From Craft to Profession: The Practice of Architecture in Nineteenth-Century America*. Berkeley: University of California Press, 1999.
Wright, Erik Olin. *Approaches to Class Analysis*. New York: Cambridge University Press, 2005.
Yates, Michael D. *Why Unions Matter*. New York: Monthly Review Press, 2009.

Notes

Preface

1. We can only hope that our historic strike is the beginning of the end of such austerity policies. Kimiko de Freytas-Tamura, "Strike Ends at the New School and Parsons School of Design," *New York Times*, December 11, 2022, https://www.nytimes.com/2022/12/11/nyregion/new-school-nyc-adjunct-strike.html.
2. Harry Braverman, *Labor and Monopoly Capital: The Degradation of Work in the Twentieth Century* (New York: Monthly Review Press, 1974), 263. Emphasis mine.
3. "If physicians can fall so precipitously, a weak profession historically tied to the marketplace like American architecture has little chance. Ever since the decline of the master artisans amid the pressures of early nineteenth-century capitalism, American building has been an increasingly competitive and fragmented market." Mary N. Woods, *From Craft to Profession: The Practice of Architecture in Nineteenth-Century America* (Berkeley: University of California Press, 1999), 178–79.

Introduction

1. U.S. Bureau of Labor Statistics, "Union Members Summary," https://www.bls.gov/news.release/union2.nr0.htm, Janurary 28, 2025.
2. Steven Greenhouse, "US Unions Winning Big Gains amid 'Great Reset' in Worker Power," *The Guardian*, October 24, 2023, https://www.theguardian.com/us-news/2023/oct/24/us-unions-successes-contracts.
3. See Gary Gerstle, *The Rise and Fall of the Neoliberal Order: America and the World in the Free Market Era* (New York: Oxford University Press, 2022).

4. Noam Scheiber, "Architects at a New York Firm Form the Industry's Only Private-Sector Union," *New York Times*, September 1, 2022.
5. Total union membership in the United States in 2022 was 14.3 million, and professional membership numbered 6.44 million in 2023. These numbers are calculated via the U.S. Bureau of Labor Statistics, "Union Members Summary," https://www.bls.gov/news.release/union2.nr0.htm, January 28, 2025; and Department for Professional Employees, AFL-CIO, "The Professional and Technical Workforce: By the Numbers," https://www.dpeaflcio.org/factsheets/the-professional-and-technical-workforce-by-the-numbers, September 01, 2024.
6. Harris Stone, *Workbook of an Unsuccessful Architect* (New York: Monthly Review Press, 1974), 176.
7. "The fact is that, for architects, the discovery of their decline as active ideologists, the awareness of the enormous technological possibilities available for rationalizing cities and territories, coupled with the daily spectacle of their waste, and the fact that specific design methods become outdated even before it is possible to verify their underlying hypotheses in reality, all create an atmosphere of anxiety." Manfredo Tafuri, *Architecture and Utopia: Design and Capitalist Development*, trans. Barbara Luigia La Penta (Cambridge, MA: MIT Press, 1976), 176.
8. Ibid., 182.
9. See Peggy Deamer and Jane Rendell, *Architecture and Labor* (New York: Routledge, Taylor & Francis Group, 2020).
10. Historian John A. Walker provides a helpful summary that also acknowledges the difficulty in pinpointing a precise definition of *design*: "Another reason why definitions are inadequate and provisional is that language, like everything else, is subject to historical change. The word 'design' has altered its meaning through time: during the Renaissance '*disegno*' (which in practice meant drawing) was considered by art theorists such as Vasari to be the basis of all the visual arts; consequently, these were often referred to as 'the arts of design.' At that time *disegno* described the inventive, conceptualizing phase which generally preceded the making of paintings, sculptures and so forth. All artists engaged in design as part of their creative activities, hence design was not yet considered the exclusive concern of a full-time professional. Designers as such only emerged later as a result of the growing specialization of functions which occurred in Europe and the United States as part of the industrial revolution of the eighteenth and nineteenth centuries. At least this is the generally accepted story." John A. Walker with Judy Attfield, *Design History and History of Design* (1989; repr., London: Pluto, 1994), 23.
11. Alberto Pérez-Gómez and Louise Pelletier, *Architectural Representation and the Perspective Hinge* (Cambridge, MA: MIT Press, 2000), 8.

12. "From the footprint of a building, construction proceeded by rhetoric and geometry, raising the elevation as discussions about the building's face continued, almost until the end. The master mason was responsible for constructing a model of the city of God on earth; but only the Architect of the Universe possessed a comprehensive foreknowledge of the project and was deemed capable of concluding the work at the end of time." Ibid., 8.
13. Francis D. K. Ching, Mark Jarzombek, and Vikramaditya Prakash, *A Global History of Architecture* (Hoboken, NJ: Wiley, 2007), 448.
14. Vitruvius, *The Ten Books of Architecture*, trans. Morris Hicky Morgan (1960; repr., New York: Dover Publications, 2020), 5.
15. "Alongside the images of eminent buildings of the past or present, and the new sets of ready-made visual models that would characterize early modern architectural books in print, another class of architectural drawings and models was fast rising to prominence: the project documents that Renaissance architects produced in growing numbers and forwarded to increasingly distant building sites—a physical distance that went hand in hand with the growing intellectual and social estrangement between architects and builders." Mario Carpo, *The Alphabet and the Algorithm* (Cambridge, MA: MIT Press, 2011), 15.
16. "This mode of production must not be considered simply as being the reproduction of the physical existence of the individuals. Rather it is a definite form of activity of these individuals, a definite form of expressing their life, a definite *mode of life* on their part. As individuals express their life, so they are. What they are, therefore, coincides with their production, both with *what* they produce and with *how* they produce. Hence what individuals are depends on the material condition of their production." Karl Marx and Friedrich Engels, *The German Ideology* (Amherst, NY: Prometheus Books, 1998), 37.
17. Even efforts to produce modular components off-site have struggled to take off. For an example, see the woefully behind schedule mega-project in Brooklyn, Atlantic Yards. It should be no surprise that the developer responsible blames unions for the failure of modular construction in this case. Norman Oder, "How Atlantic Yards Failed to Deliver Affordable Homeownership (with a Hakeem Jeffries Cameo)," *Common Edge*, January 10, 2023, https://commonedge.org/how-atlantic-yards-failed-to-deliver-affordable-homeownership-with-a-hakeem-jeffries-cameo/.
18. Mary N. Woods, *From Craft to Profession: The Practice of Architecture in Nineteenth-Century America* (Berkeley: University of California Press, 1999), 9.
19. "Throughout much of our history the loner, the self-reliant individual, the dropout, at odds with other men, appears as someone who can be respected and respect himself. The 'Americanization' of Ricca Kartides [a Greek

immigrant], for example, is the transformation of a man who once sought respect as a member of a tight-knit community into one who has sought respect from others because he can take care of himself—in other words, because he can do without them." Richard Sennett and Jonathan Cobb, *The Hidden Injuries of Class* (1972; repr., New York: W. W. Norton, 1993), 55.
20. At the beginning of the nineteenth century, "Both private and public sector works were severely undercapitalized. Banking reserves were small, and the financial system was local and fragmented. Public revenues were limited, consisting only of customs duties. The government preferred to raise funds from private sources for many public works. Private investors were adamant about short-term gains whether they financed public projects like canals and waterworks or private undertakings like speculative housing." Ibid., 21.
21. Ibid., 167.
22. Emphasis mine. Polanyi continues: "Here lay the chance of those classes which were not engaged in applying expensive, complicated, or specific machines to production. Roughly, to the landed aristocracy and the peasantry fell the task of safeguarding the martial qualities of the nation which continued to depend largely on men and soil, while the laboring people to a smaller or greater extent, became representatives of the common human interests that had become homeless. But at one time or another, each social class stood, even if unconsciously, for interests wider than its own." Karl Polanyi, *The Great Transformation: The Political and Economic Origins of Our Time* (1944; repr., Boston: Beacon Press, 2001), 139.
23. Karl Marx, tranlsated by Ben Fowkes, *Capital: A Critique of Political Economy*, vol. 1 (Harmondsworth, UK: Penguin, in association with *New Left Review*, 1990), 548.
24. Polanyi, *The Great Transformation*, 189.
25. "The crowd, a compact mass, a locus of multiple exchanges, individualities merging together, a collective effect, is abolished and replaced by a collection of separated individualities. . . . This architectural apparatus should be a machine for creating and sustaining a power relation independent of the person who exercises it." Foucault had much to say on "individualization," but though he is primarily concerned with power relations, we are concerned with worker relations. Michel Foucault, *Discipline and Punish*, 2nd ed. (New York: Vintage Books, 1995), 201.
26. "The atelier or studio entered the discourse of American practice with the architects who returned from studies at the Ecole des Beaux-Arts in Paris beginning in the 1850s. [This] gave rise to the idea of the studio as the center for architectural creativity. But the realities of American entrepreneurial practice also intruded into the studio. The association of Hunt and Richardson with the art of architecture and Ecole ateliers has obscured their

concerns with the business of architecture and the daily routines of their practices." Woods, *From Craft to Profession*, 102.

27. "In a nutshell: society and nature supply indispensable preconditions for the economy's functioning; yet the latter systematically consumes and degrades them, eventually jeopardizing its own operations. What grounds capitalism's propensity for crisis for Polanyi, then, is the inherent tendency of the 'self-regulating market' to destabilize its own conditions of possibility—through the process he calls fictitious commodification." Nancy Fraser, "Why Two Karls Are Better than One," *DFG-Kollegforscher_innengruppe Postwachstumsgesellschaften*, no. 1 (2017): 3.

28. Nancy Fraser, "A Triple Movement? Parsing the Politics of Crisis after Polanyi," *New Left Review* 81 (May 2013): 119–32, https://newleftreview.org/issues/ii81/articles/nancy-fraser-a-triple-movement, 124.

29. "What his address does is to itemise one after another the grievances felt by working people as to changes in the character of capitalist exploitation: the rise of a master-class without traditional authority or obligations; the growing distance between master and man; the transparency of the exploitation at the source of their new wealth and power; the loss of status and above all of independence for the worker, his reduction to total dependence on the master's instruments of production; the partiality of the law; the disruption of the traditional family economy; the discipline, monotony, hours, and conditions of work; loss of leisure and amenities; the reduction of the man to the status of an 'instrument.' " E. P. Thompson and Dorothy Thompson, *The Essential E..P. Thompson* (New York: Free Press, 2001), 20.

30. Ibid., 99.

31. Harry Braverman, *Labor and Monopoly Capital: The Degradation of Work in the Twentieth Century* (New York: Monthly Review Press, 1974), 92.

32. This trend could be observed with "celebrity" practices as early as the nineteenth century, with renowned offices such as McKim, Mead and White: "So esteemed was the firm that the partners could ask prospective employees for a trial period of six months to a year during which they received no pay." Woods, *From Craft to Profession*, 139.

33. Ibid., 37.

34. Braverman, *Labor and Monopoly Capital*, 10.

35. For a more detailed history of the campaign and its failures, see Isabel Ling, "Inside the Historic Union Drive at SHoP Architects," Curbed.com, February 4, 2022, https://www.curbed.com/2022/02/shop-architects-union-drive-shuts-down.html.

36. Michael Yates, *Why Unions Matter* (New York: Monthly Review Press, 2009), 42.

37. With the help of the FMCS (Federal Mediation & Conciliation Service), we

have been able to use an "enhanced collaborative" model which begins the process of defining issues collectively rather than in the rational caucus.
38. This statement was published via Architectural Workers United on September 8, 2022.
39. Our contract was ratified on July 25, 2024, https://www.archpaper.com/2024/07/union-bernheimer-architecture-ratifies-collective-bargaining-agreement/.
40. Jane McAlevey, *A Collective Bargain: Unions, Organizing, and the Fight for Democracy* (New York: HarperCollins, 2020), 244.
41. Tafuri, *Architecture and Utopia*, 182. Emphasis mine.
42. Peggy Deamer and Jane Rendell, *Architecture and Labor*, 30.

Part 1: Creative Consciousness

1. Epigraph: John Berger, *About Looking* (New York: Vintage, 1992), 72.
2. For this section an examination of the last phase is unnecessary as it is strictly concerned with observing the construction of the building and least associated with design.
3. A difficulty here is the separation between those designers who work on physical things and those whose design process remains digital from start to finish, for example, web, UX, video game, and many graphic designers. A further analysis would be required to understand the full implications of this divide. However, while the lack of physical materiality does create a real epistemological schism, an overarching similarity remains in the relationship between the author and creativity.
4. "The carpenter, lab technician, and conductor are all craftsmen because they are dedicated to good work for its own sake. Theirs is practical activity, but their labor is not simply a means to another end. The carpenter might sell more furniture if he worked faster; the technician might make do by passing the problem back to her boss; the visiting conductor might be more likely to be rehired if he watched the clock. It's certainly possible to get by in life without dedication. The craftsman represents the special human condition of being engaged." Richard Sennett, *The Craftsman* (New Haven: Yale University Press), 20. This definition is unnecessarily broad, neglecting the individual "mark" that distinguishes one person's craft from another's. Nonetheless, the observation that craft and creativity have something to do with working for good work's sake emphasizes the distinction between labor and more "enlightened" work, one Sennett adopts from his teacher Hannah Arendt via *animal laborans* vs. *homo faber*.
5. For a more robust historical definition of design, see John A. Walker and Judy Attfield, *Design History and History of Design* (1989; repr., London: Pluto, 1994).
6. Karl Marx, translated by Ben Fowkes, *Capital: A Critique of Political*

Economy, vol. 1. (Harmondsworth, UK: Penguin, in association with *New Left Review*, 1990), 284.
7. Ibid.
8. Glenn Adamson, "Do You Know Your Stuff? The Ethics of the Material World," *Aeon*, November 28, 2018, https://aeon.co/essays/do-you-know-your-stuff-the-ethics-of-the-material-world.
9. "Since the inception of Western architecture in classical Greece, the architect has not 'made' buildings; rather, he or she has made the mediating artifacts that make significant buildings possible." Alberto Pérez-Gómez and Louise Pelletier, *Architectural Representation and the Perspective Hinge* (Cambridge, MA: MIT Press, 2000), 7.
10. Tim Ingold, "The Textility of Making," *Cambridge Journal of Economics* 34/1 (2009): 91–102, https://doi.org/10.1093/cje/bep042, 92.
11. Henri Lefebvre and John Moore, *Critique of Everyday Life: The One-Volume Edition* (London ; New York: Verso, 2014), 168.
12. Samuel W. Franklin, *The Cult of Creativity: A Surprising History* (Chicago: University of Chicago Press, 2023), 17.
13. Plato: *Complete Works*, ed. John M. Cooper and D. S. Hutchinson (Indianapolis: Hackett Publishing Company, 1997), 455b. Emphasis mine.
14. I mean falseness in the sense that Georg Lukács uses the word, which does not deny the very real effects on actors of such a misguided consciousness, but "on the contrary, it requires us to investigate this 'false consciousness' concretely as an aspect of the historical totality and as a stage in the historical process." Georg Lukács, *History and Class Consciousness* (Cambridge, MA: The MIT Press, 1968), 50.
15. "Labor, land and money are essential elements of industry; they also must be organized in markets; in fact, these markets form an absolutely vital part of the economic system. But labor, land, and money are obviously *not* commodities; the postulate that anything that is bought and sold must have been produced for sale is emphatically untrue in regard to them." Karl Polanyi, *The Great Transformation: The Political and Economic Origins of Our Time* (1944; repr., Boston: Beacon Press, 2001), 75. Design defined broadly is at odds with the definition of design as a commodity, at least in the eventual forms it produces.
16. "The problem-posing educator constantly re-forms his reflections in the reflection of the students. The students—no longer docile listeners—are now critical co-investigators in dialogue with the teacher. The teacher presents the material to the students for their consideration, and reconsiders her earlier considerations as the students express their own." Paulo Freire and Myra Bergman Ramos, *Pedagogy of the Oppressed* (London: Penguin Books, 1985), 61–62.
17. As both a practicing architect and educator, I am most familiar with this

model, but I have also participated as both student and teacher in several design and art studios.

18. For example, the slope of accessible ramps or ideal building/site orientations for passive solar design.

19. According to a 2017 survey of all majors by Indiana University's National Study of Student Engagement, Architecture students work the most hours per week (22.2), followed by several kinds of Engineering majors (17.7–19.66), and Fine Arts–based majors (16.52), still well above the average of 14.96. Though stereotyped as a non-creative field, the design process, especially in terms of testing and iteration, is an integral component of engineering. Patrick Lynch, "New Survey Confirms Architecture as Most Time Consuming Major," *ArchDaily*, February 13, 2017, https://www.archdaily.com/805264/new-survey-confirms-architecture-as-most-time-consuming-major.

20. Harry Braverman, *Labor and Monopoly Capital: The Degradation of Work in the Twentieth Century* (New York: Monthly Review Press, 1974), 239–40.

21. Ibid., 294–95.

22. "Art practices are instructive because, if architects think we do art, not work, it's surprising to show that artists *do* think they do work." Peggy Deamer and Jane Rendell, *Architecture and Labor* (New York: Routledge, Taylor & Francis Group, 2020), 23.

23. Max Weber et al., *From Max Weber: Essays in Sociology* (Abingdon, UK, and New York: Routledge, 2009), 186–87.

24. Ibid., 187.

25. Ibid., 193.

26. "Above all, this differentiation evolves in such a way as to make for strict submission to the fashion that is dominant at a given time in society." Ibid., 88.

27. "Of equal importance to the exclusionary right of property is that set of closure practices sometimes referred to as 'credentialism'—that is, the inflated use of educational certificates as a means of monitoring entry to key positions in the division of labor." Frank Parkin, *Marxism and Class Theory: A Bourgeois Critique* (London: Tavistock Publications, 1981), 54.

28. Ibid., 54.

29. The first state to grant licensure to architects was Illinois in 1897. NCARB (National Council of Architectural Registration Boards), "Beginning of Licensure," NCARB Centennial, 2018.

30. Ibid., 57.

31. Lukács, *History and Class Consciousness*, 52.

32. Ibid., 46.

33. "One of the most fraught consequences is the separation of the economic struggle from the political one." Ibid., 70–71. While the ultimate goal is

indeed to achieve real concrete change, we must begin with the economic struggle, as it is in its most early stages within design professions.
34. Ibid., 83.
35. Ibid., 98. Emphasis mine.
36. Apple, "Think Different," *YouTube*, September 30, 2013.
37. See Richard Florida, *Rise of the Creative Class* (New York: Basic Books, 2002).
38. Lukács, *History and Class Consciousness*, 50.
39. "During the second period of the labour process, that in which his labour is no longer necessary labour, the worker does indeed expend labour-power, he does work, but his labour is no longer necessary labour, and he creates no value for himself. He creates surplus-value which, for the capitalist, has all the charms of something created out of nothing. This part of the working day I call surplus labour-time, and to the labour expended during that time I have the name of surplus labour." Marx, *Capital*, vol. 1, 325.
40. Because I am most familiar with the sector, and architecture firms tend to be associated quite strongly with traditional "business," I utilized the AIA (American Institute of Architects) data to understand profit margins in a typical design profession. For example, according to the 2015 firm benchmark, just over 50 percent of firms reported either being "modestly profitable" or "reporting loss." In 2013, this percentage was almost 60 percent, and in 2011 it was even worse: 65 percent. American Institute of Architects, "Firm Benchmarking Tool—AIA," https://www.aia.org/firmbenchmarkingtool.
41. Marx, *Capital*, vol. 1, 325.
42. Verónica Gago and Liz Mason-Deese, *Feminist International: How to Change Everything* (London and New York: Verso, 2020), 124.
43. Graduates with a bachelor's degree in design fields have debt that ranges from $12,000 to $30,000, and those with Master's range from $23,000 to $100,000. The situation is on the high end for architects with graduate degrees but far worse for those with a bachelor's degree: according to a survey by the AIA, "The average student loan debt among graduates with a five-year bachelor's degree comes in at $42,000, while the average debt for those who earn a master's in architecture tops $72,000." Melanie Hanson, "Student Loan Debt by Major [2022]: Highest + Lowest Average Debt," Education Data Initiative, https://educationdata.org/student-loan-debt-by-major, August 28, 2024; and Korey White, "Student Loan Forgiveness, Repayment Programs Are Critical—AIA," https://www.aia.org/articles/6646112-student-loan-forgiveness-repayment-program, July 11, 2023. [original article for AIA was removed but a record exists here: https://content.aia.org/node/6646112].
44. After we achieved voluntary recognition for BA Union, the Principal of our office, Andy Bernheimer, did something unprecedented for a firm owner.

During an AIA awards ceremony, he began his presentation by acknowledging every member of the office verbally and visually, noting their individual contributions to the projects he was sharing with the audience. While it was typical in the sense that the owner (and not the workers) was receiving the award, what was atypical was the specific recognition of the collective labor involved. While a relatively small moment, shifts like this can be powerful acts in the building of a new class consciousness.

45. Erik Olin Wright, *Approaches to Class Analysis* (Cambridge and New York: Cambridge University Press, 2006), 29.
46. Chris Walton, "Workers at Snøhetta Vote against Unionization," *The Architect's Newspaper*, July 7, 2023. Workers at offices such as Snøhetta often appeal to a "third way" since they believe their places of work make them special, while the reality is they are workers just like everyone else.
47. Pierre Bourdieu, "The Social Space and the Genesis of Groups," *Theory and Society* 14/6 (November 1985): 208.
48. Braverman, *Labor and Monopoly Capital*, 284. Emphasis mine.
49. "The proletarian is endowed with fundamental health and a sense of reality which other social groups lose in so far as they become detached from practical creative activity." Lefebvre and Moore. *Critique of Everyday Life*, 163.
50. Adamson, "Do You Know Your Stuff?"
51. See Mario Carpo, *The Alphabet and the Algorithm* (Cambridge, MA: MIT Press, 2011).
52. Marx, *Capital*, vol. 1, 547.
53. "As historians, [Marx and Engels] refused to be idle onlookers of history.... They were the first to perceive how thought is linked to *action*. They were able to get to the very roots of ideas, to the fundamental questions. With Marx and Engels philosophical thought at its most coherent and most methodical comes down to the level of life and it penetrates it, it reveals it." Lefebvre and Moore, *Critique of Everyday Life*, 162.
54. Matthew Stewart, "The Birth of the New American Aristocracy," *The Atlantic*, May 16, 2018), https://www.theatlantic.com/magazine/archive/2018/06/the-birth-of-a-new-american-aristocracy/559130/.
55. "In countries where modern civilisation has become fully developed, a new class of petty bourgeois has been formed, fluctuating between proletariat and bourgeoisie, and ever renewing itself as a supplementary part of bourgeois society. The individual members of this class, however, are being constantly hurled down into the proletariat by the action of competition, and, as modern industry develops, they even see the moment approaching when they will completely disappear as an independent section of modern society, to be replaced in manufactures, agriculture and commerce, by overlookers, bailiffs and shopmen." Karl Marx and Friedrich Engels, *The Communist Manifesto* (1888; repr., London: Penguin, 2002), 247. While

as a class they were diminishing, Marx and Engels did not foresee how the *social identity* of the petty bourgeoisie in relation to status would remain throughout intense periods of economic change.

56. C. Wright Mills, *White Collar: The American Middle Classes* (London: Andesite Press, 2015), xvi.
57. "This symbolic manipulation of groups finds a paradigmatic form in political strategies: thus, by virtue of their objective position situated halfway between the two poles of the space, standing in a state of unstable equilibrium and wavering between two opposed alliances, the occupants of the intermediate positions of the social field are the object of completely contradictory classifications by those who try, in the political struggle, to win them over to their side." Pierre Bourdieu, "What Makes a Social Class? On the Theoretical and Practical Existence of Groups," *Berkeley Journal of Sociology* 32 (1987): 1–17, 12.
58. Mills, *White Collar*, xii.
59. "While every worker is a wage earner, not every wage earner is a worker, since not every wage earner is necessarily a productive worker, i.e. one who produces surplus value (commodities)." Nicos Poulantzas, "On Social Classes," *New Left Review* 1/78 (March 1973): 27–54, 30–31.
60. Ibid., 35.
61. Mary N. Woods, *From Craft to Profession: The Practice of Architecture in Nineteenth-Century America* (Berkeley: University of California Press, 1999), 32–37.
62. The Center for Architecture in New York City, a local chapter of the national AIA, held one event that loosely embraced the conversation.
63. Christopher D. Green, "Classics in the History of Psychology—A. H. Maslow (1943), *A Theory of Human Motivation*," Yorku.ca, 2019, http://psychclassics.yorku.ca/Maslow/motivation.htm.

Part 2: Class Consciousness

1. Epigraph: Hannah Arendt, *The Human Condition*, 2nd ed. (Chicago: University of Chicago Press, 1958).
2. Karl Marx and Friedrich Engels, *The Communist Manifesto* (London: Penguin, 2002), 231.
3. Noam Scheiber, "Architects at a New York Firm Form the Industry's Only Private-Sector Union," *New York Times*, September 1, 2022.
4. Marx and Engels, *The Communist Manifesto*, 222.
5. While this is universally true in economic terms, there are certain workers who while exploited economically still primarily serve the interests of the ruling class. Employees such as clerks for judges, prison guards, venture capitalists staffers, and others can be distinguished from the class consciousness we are focusing on. Though some designers take on work that also

fits in this categorizations, like the design of prisons or luxury watches, on the whole designers are primarily interested with servicing basic needs and goods for the general populace. For more on this distinction, see Michael Yates, *Can the Working Class Change the World?* (New York: Monthly Review Press, 2018), chap. 1.
6. Erik Olin Wright, *Approaches to Class Analysis* (New York: Cambridge University Press, 2005), 15.
7. Erik Olin Wright, "Ch 8: Class Analysis." *Social Class and Stratification: Classic Statements and Theoretical Debates*, ed. Rhonda Levine (Lanham: Rowman & Littlefield, 2006). 4.
8. Wright, *Approaches to Class Analysis*, 18.
9. Ibid., 23.
10. Ibid., 24.
11. The distinction here is between exploitation based on wage labor and expropriation based on coerced labor and outright theft. The latter case is evident in the example of stolen Native American lands that Wright references, but also includes employment that does not compensate enough to provide an adequate living and/or is actively physically and mentally harmful to the worker, the most extreme case being chattel slavery as practiced in the United States. Both categories exclude reproductive labor, i.e., the raising of children, which is typically wholly uncompensated but critical for the perpetuation of the economy. Though outside of our analysis for obvious reasons, it is important to note that capitalism cannot function without all three of these categories, and indeed was only possible through a combination of all of them. For more on expropriation, see Yates, *Can the Working Class Change the World?*; and Nancy Fraser, "Behind Marx's Hidden Abode: For an Expanded Conception of Capitalism," *New Left Review* 86 (March–April 2014).
12. Wright, *Approaches to Class Analysis*, 25.
13. Ibid., 25.
14. Georg Lukács, *History and Class Consciousness* (Cambridge, MA: The MIT Press, 1968), 59–60.
15. Unionization in this context only continues to support the needs of an enclosed group of privileged individuals, rather than connecting with other groups and struggles.
16. Max Weber et al., *From Max Weber: Essays in Sociology* (New York: Routledge, 2009), 191.
17. "When the worker knows himself as a commodity his knowledge is practical. *That is to say, this knowledge brings about an objective structural change in the object of knowledge.*" Lukács, *History and Class Consciousness*, 169.
18. Erik Olin Wright, "The Shadow of Exploitation in Weber's Class Analysis," *American Sociological Review* 67/6 (December 2002): 850.

19. Ibid., 851.
20. William Morris, *Useful Work v. Useless Toil* (London and New York: Penguin Books, 2008), 4. Emphasis mine.
21. Ibid., 60–61.
22. As is the case with Foxconn workers in China who committed suicide due to the deplorable working conditions "necessary" to create the chips for Apple products. See Brian Merchant, *The One Device: The Secret History of the iPhone* (New York: Back Bay Books, 2018).
23. New York State Department of Labor, "Introduction to the Prevailing Rate Schedule," October 1, 2023, https://apps.labor.ny.gov/wpp/viewPrevailingWageSchedule.do?typeid=1&county=91.
24. Michael Yates, *Why Unions Matter* (New York: Monthly Review Press, 2009), 190.
25. William Morris, *Useful Work v. Useless* Toil, 51.
26. Maureen Dowd, "Opinion: Watch Out for the Fake Tom Cruise," *New York Times*, July 15, 2023.
27. See Karl Kinsella, *God's Own Language* (Cambridge, MA: MIT Press, 2023), for relatively new research into the relatively unknown story of twelfth-century theologian Hugh of Saint Victor's inchoate foray into architectural drawing. At a minimum, we can date the origins of modern architectural drawing to Alberti in the Renaissance, approximately 600 years ago
28. "On the one hand, it is emphasized that modern work, as a result of the scientific-technical revolution and 'automation,' requires ever higher levels of education, training, the greater exercise of intelligence and mental effort in general. At the same time, a mounting dissatisfaction with the condition of industrial and office labor appears to contradict this view." Harry Braverman, *Labor and Monopoly Capital: The Degradation of Work in the Twentieth Century* (New York: Monthly Review Press, 1974), 3.
29. VentureBeat, "Pirros, a Startup that Applies AI to Streamline Drawing Sets for Buildings and Infrastructure, Lands $2 Million Seed Round," VentureBeat, August 31, 2023, https://venturebeat.com/ai/pirros-a-startup-that-applies-ai-to-streamline-drawing-sets-for-buildings-and-infrastructure-lands-2-million-seed-round/.
30. Writers Guild of America, "Summary of the 2023 WGA MBA," September 2023, https://www.wgacontract2023.org/the-campaign/summary-of-the-2023-wga-mba?utm_source=substack&utm_medium=email.
31. I am indebted to the contribution of Je Siqueira for this section, particularly in the research behind the UTOPIA project. See our original writing on the UTOPIA project: Chris Beck and Je Siqueira, "What the Bernheimer Architecture Union Learned from UTOPIA," *The Architect's Newspaper*, October 13, 2023.

32. Rob Howard, "UTOPIA: Where Workers Craft New Technology," *Technology Review* 88 (April 1985).
33. Ibid.
34. "Little programs are delightful to write in isolation, but the process of maintaining large-scale software is always miserable. Because of this, digital technology tempts the programmer's psyche into a kind of schizophrenia. There is constant confusion between real and ideal computers. Technologists wish every program behaved like a brand-new, playful little program, and will use any available psychological strategy to avoid thinking about computers realistically. The brittle character of maturing computer programs can cause digital designs to get frozen into place by a process known as lock-in. This happens when many software programs are designed to work with an existing one. The process of significantly changing software in a situation in which a lot of other software is dependent on it is the hardest thing to do. So it almost never happens." Jaron Lanier, *You Are Not a Gadget: A Manifesto* (New York: Vintage Books, 2011), 7.
35. See Christian Berggren, *Alternatives to Lean Production: Work Organization in the Swedish Auto Industry* (1992; repr., Ithaca, NY: Cornell University Press, 2019). One important observation among many: "During the three years Volvo Uddevalla was in operation, productivity (assembly hours per car) improved by more than 50 percent. From the last quarter of 1990 to the last quarter of 1992, the plant cut the assembly time at an average rate of one hour per month. By mid-1991 Uddevalla's performance equaled that of Gothenburg' s assembly line. From then on both plants improved rapidly, but Uddevalla had an edge. Furthermore, its rate of improvement was particularly high in the second half of 1992, when a new management introduced a radical, process-oriented, flat organization, made up of only two hierarchical levels. None of its managers doubted that the plant could reach the target rate of 25 hours per car by mid-1993. (Interestingly, within Uddevalla there were no significant differences between the larger assembly teams working in long cycles of 1.5 hours and mini-teams working in very long cycles of 7 hours.)" (viii).
36. Ibid., 146.
37. Ibid., 149.
38. "When the training shop opened in 1986, the manager in charge formulated the goal as follows: 'In the training shop we learn how to make complete cars. Both manual and intellectual functions are required: planning, organizing equipment and materials, assembling, following up, and reporting. Assembly here involves more than just mounting screws; it's also a matter of functional know-how.'" Ibid., 150.
39. "There was an appreciable reduction of physical strains, thanks to the production design and efforts in the area of ergonomics, and fourth, group

cooperation was the basis for administrative delegation and self-regulation of the work but also a means of exerting peer pressure to reach production targets and be given the productivity bonus." Ibid., 162.

40. Braverman, *Labor and Monopoly Capital*, 133.
41. Berggren, *Alternatives to Lean Production*, 149–50.
42. Camila Domonoske, "GM Autoworkers Approve New Contract, Securing Wage Increases," NPR, November 16, 2023, https://www.npr.org/2023/11/16/1212381342/gm-autoworkers-vote-yes-approve-uaw-contract-ford-stellantis.
43. I was a part-time faculty member walking on the picket line during this strike.
44. Writers Guild of America, "Summary of the 2023 WGA MBA," https://www.wga.org/contracts/contracts/mba/summary-of-the-2023-wga-mba.
45. John Koblin, "Hollywood Writers Ratify New Contract with Studios," *New York Times*, October 9, 2023, https://www.nytimes.com/2023/10/09/business/media/screenwriters-contract-ratify.html.
46. Writers Guild of America, "Summary of the 2023 WGA MBA."
47. Brooks Barnes, John Koblin, and Nicole Sperling, "Striking Actors and Hollywood Studios Agree to a Deal," *New York Times*, November 9, 2023, https://www.nytimes.com/2023/11/08/business/media/actors-strike-deal.html.
48. Alex N. Press, "Workers Have Won the First Union at a Major US Video Game Company," *Jacobin*, May 24, 2022, https://jacobin.com/2022/05/activision-blizzard-union-video-game-workers-warcraft-call-duty.
49. Karl Polanyi, *The Great Transformation: The Political and Economic Origins of Our Time* (1944; repr., Boston: Beacon Press, 2001), 139.
50. Ibid., 139. Emphasis mine.
51. Here we can summarize much of the argument up to this point, via Wright, that designers are in fact exploited workers, but also occupy a "class location" which is "not 'a class'; it is a location-within-relation." Wright, *Approaches to Class Analysis*, 19. This is the context in which I used the word "privilege."
52. Marx and Engels, *The Communist Manifesto*, 229. Emphasis mine.
53. Marx, *Capital*, vol. 1, 284.
54. "The most important life activities have consistently been held by the powers that be to be unworthy of those who are fully human most centrally because of their close connections with necessity and life: motherwork (the rearing of children), housework, and until the rise of capitalism in the West, any work necessary to subsistence. In addition, these activities in contemporary capitalism are all constructed in ways which systematically degrade and destroy the minds and bodies of those who perform them." Nancy C.M. Hartsock, "Ch 3: The Feminist Standpoint: Developing the Ground

for a Specifically Feminist Historical Materialism." *The Feminist Standpoint Theory Reader: Intellectual and Political Controversies*, ed. Sandra Harding (New York: Routledge, 2004), 48.

55. "[Abraham Lincoln] was enunciating the widespread American idea of the son rising to a higher economic level than the father; of the chance for the poor man to accumulate wealth and power, which made the European doctrine of a working class fighting for the elevation of all workers seem not only less desirable but even less possible for average workers than they had formerly considered it." W. E. B. Du Bois, *Black Reconstruction in America* (1935; repr., New York: Free Press, 1998), 18.

56. "[Financialized capitalism] is a deeply predatory and unstable form of social organization that liberates capital accumulation from the very constraints (political, ecological, social, moral) needed to sustain it over time. Freed from such constraints, capitalism's economy consumes its own background conditions of possibility. It is like a tiger that eats its own tail." Nancy Fraser, *The Old Is Dying and the New Cannot Be Born* (New York: Verso Books, 2019), 37–38.

57. "But abolitionists, feminists, and anti-colonialists were hardly partisans of the 'self-regulating market,' as they also opposed market-mediated modes of domination, such as super-exploitation, unequal exchange, and the imperialism of free trade. Situated on neither side of Polanyi's double movement, they occupied a third position, obscured by his analysis, a position I have called *emancipation* ... these movements sought instead to overcome domination across the board, in society as well as economy." Fraser, "Why Two Karls are Better than One," 8.

Together We Build

1. Epigraph: Ursula K Le Guin, *The Language of the Night: Essays on Fantasy and Science Fiction* (New York: Perigee, 1980).
2. National Council of Architectural Registration Boards, "NBTN 2023 Demographics," June 26, 2023, https://www.ncarb.org/nbtn2023/demographics.
3. Data USA, "Graphic Designers: Data USA," https://datausa.io/profile/soc/graphic-designers#occupation-by-industry. Based on U.S. Census Bureau data.
4. An event hosted by the AIA featured an image of a child unwittingly dragged to a construction site, in which mothers are given tools to relieve the symptoms of an economic system that puts the cost of reproductive labor squarely on women and parents. AIA New York, "Women in Architecture Forum: Practice and Motherhood," Calendar, October 13, 2023, https://calendar.aiany.org/2023/11/09/aiany-women-in-architecture-forum-practice-and-motherhood/.

5. "The Great Acceleration is reaching criticality. Enormous, immediate challenges confront humanity over the next few decades as it attempts to pass through a bottleneck of continued population growth, excessive resource use, and environmental deterioration. In most parts of the world the demand for fossil fuels overwhelms the desire to significantly reduce greenhouse gas emissions. About 60% of ecosystem services are already degraded and will continue to degrade further unless significant societal changes in values and management occur." Will Steffen, Paul J. Crutzen, and John R. McNeill, "The Anthropocene: Are Humans Now Overwhelming the Great Forces of Nature?," *Ambio* 36/8 (December 2007): 614–21, 620.
6. John Bellamy Foster, "Marx's Theory of Metabolic Rift: Classical Foundations for Environmental Sociology," *American Journal of Sociology* 105/2 (September 1999): 366–405, at 400.
7. "Today, Nancy Fraser may fairly be called the leading socialist feminist of the Anglophone world." Caitlín Doherty, "Topographies of Capital," *New Left Review* 143 (October 12, 2023): 31–52, https://newleftreview.org/issues/ii143/articles/caitlin-doherty-topographies-of-capital.
8. Fraser, "A Triple Movement? Parsing the Politics of Crisis after Polanyi," 122.
9. Nancy Fraser, "From Redistribution to Recognition? Dilemmas of Justice in a 'Post-Socialist' Age," *New Left Review* 1/212 (July 1995): 68–93.
10. Ibid., 74.
11. Ibid., 78.
12. Ibid., 79.
13. Ibid., 80.
14. Ibid., 87.
15. "The long-term goal of deconstructive feminism is a culture in which hierarchical gender dichotomies are replaced by networks of multiple intersecting differences that are demassified and shifting. This goal is consistent with transformative socialist-feminist redistribution. Deconstruction opposes the sort of sedimentation or congealing of gender difference that occurs in an unjustly gendered political economy. Its utopian image of a culture in which ever new constructions of identity and difference are freely elaborated and then swiftly deconstructed is only possible, after all, on the basis of rough social equality." Ibid., 89–90.
16. "The planners and local councillors who make and apply these rules are, like architects, usually male. They do not necessarily promote their own interest at the expense of women's, but they may not have considered whether different sections of the population have different environmental needs. Lack of consideration may show itself at all levels of decision-making, from the layout of kitchens in council houses, or public buildings made inaccessible to people with prams or wheelchairs, to the whole relationship

between home, workplace and other facilities which may affect women differently to men. Women's voices are not heard during this decision-making process which is supposed to ensure that building development takes place in a socially responsible way. When both the client and the local authority are satisfied with the architect's proposal, arrangements will be made to build the scheme, using an almost all-male workforce. In short, women play almost no part in making decisions about or in creating the environment. It is a *man-made* environment." Matrix, *Making Space : Women and the Man-Made Environment* (London: Pluto Press, 1985), 3.
17. Ibid., 5.
18. "In this way, we also put another idea of productivity into play: productivity is not confirmed by whether or not we are exploited under the wage form. Rather, the reasoning is different: the form of exploitation organized by the wage invisibilizes, disciplines, and hierarchizes other forms of exploitation." Verónica Gago and Liz Mason-Deese, *Feminist International: How to Change Everything* (London and New York: Verso, 2020), 53.
19. Ibid., 144.
20. "The form of the strike's organization produces transversality. In so doing, it updates those historical lines of struggle and projects them onto a feminism of the masses. This feminism is rooted in concrete struggles of popular economy workers, migrants, cooperative workers, precarious workers, women defending their territories, new generations of sexual dissidents, housewives who refuse enclosure, those fighting for the right to abortion in a broad struggle for bodily autonomy, mobilized students, women denouncing agrotoxins, and sex workers, among others. In organizational terms, it creates a common horizon that functions as a practical catalyst." Ibid., 208.
21. Ibid., 14.
22. Ibid., 20.
23. W. E. B. Du Bois, *Black Reconstruction in America* (1935; repr., New York: Free Press, 1998), 5.
24. Ibid., 9.
25. Ibid., 17.
26. "Then they began to see a way out for the worker in America through the free land of the West. Here was a solution such as was impossible in Europe; plenty of land, rich land, land coming daily nearer its own markets, to which the worker could retreat and restore the industrial balance ruined in Europe by expropriation of the worker from the soil." Ibid., 19.
27. Ibid., 67.
28. "'Race,' too, therefore, is a bivalent mode of collectivity with both a political-economic and a cultural-valuational, face. Its two faces intertwine to reinforce one another dialectically, as racist and Eurocentric cultural norms

are institutionalized in the state and the economy, while the economic disadvantage suffered by people of colour restricts their 'voice.' *Redressing racial injustice, therefore, requires changing both political economy and culture.*" Nancy Fraser, "From Redistribution to Recognition? Dilemmas of Justice in a 'Post-Socialist' Age," 81. Emphasis mine.

29. Michael Sainato, "'We Want Everybody Walking Out': UAW Chief Outlines Mass Strike for May 2028," *The Guardian*, January 22, 2024, sec. US news, https://www.theguardian.com/us-news/2024/jan/22/autoworkers-uaw-shawn-fain-may-2028-national-strike.

30. See Heather C. McGhee, *The Sum of Us: What Racism Costs Everyone and How We Can Prosper Together* (New York: One World, 2021).

31. United States Environmental Protection Agency, "Sources of Greenhouse Gas Emissions," October 5, 2023, https://www.epa.gov/ghgemissions/sources-greenhouse-gas-emissions.

32. "Analytic frameworks engaging questions of freedom by way of critiques of capitalist globalization have not, in any way, become obsolete in the age of climate change. If anything, as Davis shows, climate change may well end up accentuating all the inequities of the capitalist world order if the interests of the poor and vulnerable are neglected . . . Capitalist globalization exists; so should its critiques. But these critiques do not give us an adequate hold on human history once we accept that the crisis of climate change is here with us and may exist as part of this planet for much longer than capitalism or long after capitalism has undergone many more historic mutations. The problematic of globalization allows us to read climate change only as a crisis of capitalist management. While there is no denying that climate change has profoundly to do with the history of capital, a critique that is only a critique of capital is not sufficient for addressing questions relating to human history once the crisis of climate change has been acknowledged and the Anthropocene has begun to loom on the horizon of our present. The geologic now of the Anthropocene has become entangled with the now of human history." Dipesh Chakrabarty, "The Climate of History: Four Theses," *Critical Inquiry* 35/ 2 (January 2009): 197–222, https://doi.org/10.1086/596640., 212.

33. René Descartes, *The Philosophical Writings of Descartes,* vol. 1, trans. John Cottingham, Robert Stoothoff, and Dugald Murdoch (1985; repr., New York: Cambridge University Press, 2006), 9.

34. Lorraine Daston, "Baconian Facts, Academic Civility and the Prehistory of Objectivity," *Annals of Scholarship* 8 (1991): 37–63, 40–44.

35. Ibid., 45.

36. Amitav Ghosh, *The Nutmeg's Curse: Parables for a Planet in Crisis* (Chicago: University of Chicago Press, 2022), 37.

37. Robin Wall Kimmerer, *Braiding Sweetgrass: Indigenous Wisdom, Scientific*

Knowledge and the Teachings of Plants (Minneapolis: Milkweed Editions, 2013), 44.
38. Descartes, e.g. "Rule Seven," 25.
39. Ghosh, *The Nutmeg's Curse*, 35–36.
40. Hazel Clark and David Brody, *Design Studies: A Reader* (2009; repr., UK: Bloomsbury Academic, 2016), 1.
41. John Bellamy Foster, "Marx's Theory of Metabolic Rift: Classical Foundations for Environmental Sociology," *American Journal of Sociology* 105/2 (September 1999): 383.
42. "For Marx, the 'excrement produced by man's natural metabolism,' along with the waste of industrial production and consumption, needed to be recycled back into the production, as part of a complete metabolic cycle." Foster, "Marx's Theory of Metabolic Rift," 384.
43. See Richard Campanella, *Bienville's Dilemma: A Historical Geography of New Orleans* (Lafayette, LA: Center for Louisiana Studies, University of Louisiana at Lafayette, 2008). Campanella's geographical history of New Orleans is one of the most thorough, drawing fascinating connections between the natural development of the land and current demographic configurations of the city.
44. See Campanella's illuminating maps in *Bienville's Dilemma*.
45. Olúfẹ́mi O. Táíwò, *Reconsidering Reparations* (New York: Oxford University Press, 2022), 157.
46. Maria Mies and Vandana Shiva, *Ecofeminism* (London and New York: Zed Books, 2014), 72.
47. Ibid., 72.
48. bell hooks, *Belonging: A Culture of Place* (New York: Routledge, 2009), 7.
49. "Leaving the agrarian past meant leaving cultures of belonging and community wherein resources were shared for a culture of liberal individualism. There is very little published work that looks at the psychological turmoil black folks faced as they made serious geographical changes that brought with them new psychological demands." Ibid., 22.
50. "New York City was one of the few places in the world where I experienced loneliness for the first time. I attributed this to the fact that there one lives in close proximity to so many people engaging in a kind of pseudo intimacy but rarely genuinely making community. To live in close contact with neighbors, to see them every day but never to engage in fellowship was downright depressing. People I knew in the city often ridiculed the idea that one would want to live in community—what they loved about the city was the intense anonymity, not knowing and not being accountable." Ibid., 24.
51. Though these data are state level, it is not difficult to extract the fact that states with larger cities within their borders consume far less energy than largely rural states: New York, the second-lowest consuming state,

consumes 178 million Btu per capita per year, and California 189 million Btu, while states like Wyoming and North Dakota emit 870 million Btu and 905 million Btu, respectively. See U.S. Energy Information Administration, "U.S. States – Rankings: U.S. Energy Information Administration (EIA)," 2016, https://www.eia.gov/state/rankings/. An analytical connection can be found here: https://www.theguardian.com/us-news/2021/aug/22/cities-climate-change-dense-sprawl-yimby-nimby

52. hooks, *Belonging: A Culture of Place*, 26.
53. Foster, "Marx's Theory of Metabolic Rift," 397.
54. Ibid., 400.
55. Kimmerer, *Braiding Sweetgrass*, 45.
56. "The left too has its taboos to give up. They include deep-seated hostility to nuclear power, aversion to centralized solar power plants and other large-scale infrastructure, and blanket rejection of any talk of geoengineering. The latter is no longer a tenable position, if it ever was; not long after climate change emerged as a problem, it became clear that CO_2 concentrations would need to be reduced to, for example, 350 ppm, as proposed by 350.org." Andreas Malm, "Planning the Planet," in *Has It Come to This?: The Promises and Perils of Geoengineering on the Brink*, ed. J. P. Sapinski, Holly Jean Buck, and Andreas Malm (New Brunswick, NJ: Rutgers University Press, 2020), 157.
57. "The human interaction with nature always had to take the form of a metabolic cycle that needed to be sustained for the sake of successive generations. Technological improvements were a necessary but insufficient means for the 'improvement' in the human relation to the earth. For Marx, human beings transformed their relation to nature but not exactly as they pleased; they did so in accordance with conditions inherited from the past and as a result of a complex process of historical development that reflected a changing relation to a natural world, which was itself dynamic in character." Foster, "Marx's Theory of Metabolic Rift," 390.
58. Ghosh, *The Nutmeg's Curse*, 102. Emphasis mine.
59. Liza Featherstone, "Autoworkers' Historic Victory Is a Turning Point in the Climate Culture War," *The New Republic*, November 3, 2023, https://newrepublic.com/article/176602/auto-workers-historic-victory-turning-point-climate-culture-war.
60. Laura Anaya-Morga, "Caltrans Projected to Break Ground on Wildlife Bridge Over 101 Freeway in January 2022," *Los Angeles Times*, October 9, 2021, https://www.latimes.com/california/story/2021-10-09/caltrans-wildlife-bridge-101-freeway-agoura-hills-january-2022.
61. Maya Yang, "'Super Exciting' Visit of Dolphins to East River Offers Hope of Cleaner New York," *The Guardian*, February 24, 2025, https://www.theguardian.com/us-news/2025/feb/24/dolphins-new-york-east-river-environment.

Conclusion: What Is the Architecture of Labor?

1. Epigraph: William Morris, *Useful Work v. Useless Toil* (London and New York: Penguin Books, 2008).
2. David Harvey, *Rebel Cities: From the Right to the City to the Urban Revolution* (2012; repr., Brooklyn, NY: Verso, 2019), 89.
3. Ibid., 112.
4. "The chances of classes in a struggle will depend upon their ability to win support from outside their own membership. Which again will depend upon their fulfillment of tasks set by interests wider than their own. Thus neither the birth nor the death of classes, neither their aims nor the degree to which they attain them; neither their cooperations nor their antagonisms can be understood apart from the interests of society, given by its situation as a whole." Karl Polanyi, *The Great Transformation: The Political and Economic Origins of Our Time* (1944; repr., Boston: Beacon Press, 2001), 59.
5. "The Radical and free-thinking artisan was at his most earnest in his belief in the active duties of citizenship. Moreover, together with this sobriety, the artisan culture nurtured the values of intellectual enquiry and of mutuality. We have seen much of the first quality, displayed in the fight for press freedom. The autodidact had often an uneven, laboured understanding, but it was his own. Since he had been forced to find his intellectual way, he took little on trust: his mind did not move within the established ruts of a formal education. Many of his ideas challenged authority, and authority had tried to suppress them." E. P. Thompson and Dorothy Thompson, *The Essential E.P. Thompson* (New York: Free Press, 2001), 99.
6. "I am seeking to rescue the poor stockinger, the Luddite cropper, the 'obsolete' hand-loom weaver, the 'utopian' artisan, and even the deluded follower of Joanna Southcott, from the enormous condescension of posterity. Their crafts and traditions may have been dying. Their hostility to the new industrialism may have been backward-looking. Their communitarian ideals may have been fantasies. Their insurrectionary conspiracies may have been foolhardy. But they lived through these times of acute social disturbance, and we did not. Their aspirations were valid in terms of their own experience, and, if they were casualties of history, they remain, condemned in their own lives, as casualties." Ibid., 6.
7. Michael D. Yates, *Why Unions Matter* (New York: Monthly Review Press, 2009), 198.
8. Ibid.
9. Allison Rudnick, "The Art of the Great Depression," Metropolitan Museum of Art, September 18, 2023, https://www.metmuseum.org/perspectives/articles/2023/9/the-art-of-the-great-depression.
10. Olúfẹ́mi O. Táíwò, *Reconsidering Reparations* (New York: Oxford University Press, 2022), 189.

11. For example, here in New York State we have the New York Power Authority, the largest such public utility in the United States and which also has origins in the New Deal era. While effective at delivering lower-cost electricity with no profit motive, and even serving as the original model for other similar agencies, it could learn from the ambitious all-encompassing approach of the historical TVA.
12. Jerusalem Demsas, "Why Does It Cost so Much to Build Things in America?," Vox, June 28, 2021, https://www.vox.com/22534714/rail-roads-infrastructure-costs-america.
13. See Christine Macy, "The Architect's Office of Tennessee Valley Authority," in *The Tennessee Valley Authority: Design and Persuasion*, ed. Tim Culvahouse (New York: Princeton Architectural Press, 2007).
14. See Barry M. Katz, "Ideology and Engineering in the Tennessee Valley," in Culvahouse, *The Tennessee Valley Authority: Design and Persuasion*.
15. Wisconsin Historical Society, "Milwaukee Sewer Socialism, Turning Points in Wisconsin History, Wisconsin Historical Society," n.d., https://www.wisconsinhistory.org/turningpoints/tp-043/?action=more_essay.
16. A term rediscovered and popularized by economist Adam Tooze. See Kate Whiting and HyoJin Park, "We're in a 'Polycrisis'— a Historian Explains What That Means," World Economic Forum, March 7, 2023, https://www.weforum.org/stories/2023/03/polycrisis-adam-tooze-historian-explains/.

Index

actors, strike by, 96, 98, 106–7
Adamson, Glenn, 49–50, 76
Adobe (firm), 94, 95, 98
Alberti, Leon Battista, 23
alienation: in design process, 59; Mills on, 79; of workers in auto industry, 103
American Institute of Architects (AIA), 81
Apple (firm), 51, 67, 74
architectural drawings, 97
Architectural Workers United (AWU), 34, 36, 112
architecture: contemporary problems in, 29–32; demographics of, 111; historical development in U.S. of, 25–27; professionalization of, 63–64; since Renaissance, 22–23; specialization within, 76–83; Stone on history of, 20–21; unionization in, 34–37, 86
architecture studios, 43, 56–57
Arendt, Hannah, 84
Argentina, 116–18
Aristotle, 50–51
artificial intelligence (AI), 96, 98; strike of writers and actors over, 106–7
Autodesk (firm), 32, 95, 97, 98
automation, 96
auto workers, 99, 101–6

Bacon, Francis, 123–24
Bell, Daniel, 140
Bentham, Jeremy, 28
Berger, John, 42
Berggren, Christian, 102

INDEX

Bernheimer Architecture (BA; firm), 33–39, 99
BIM (Building Information Modeling; software), 32, 94, 97
Blacks: Great Migration of, 131; as workers, 119–20
Bourdieu, Pierre, 74
Braverman, Harry: on automation, 103; on craft, 32; on office workers, 58; on productive and unproductive labor, 74–75; on technical workers, 16
Brody, David, 126
building industry, 114, 115
buildings, heating of, 130–31, 136–37

capitalism, status of designers in, 68
Carpo, Mario, 77
cars: auto workers, 101; reorganization of production of, 101–6
cities, 140
Clark, Hazel, 126
class: Lukács on, 65; status versus, 62–63
class conflict, 14
class consciousness: Du Bois on, 119; Lukács on, 65; status consciousness and, 68
climate change, 122–23

computer-aided drawing (CAD), 96, 97
Condé Nast Union, 143
Congress of Industrial Organizations (CIO), 142–43
consciousness: creative consciousness, 61–68; Lukács on, 88–89
construction, 81–82, 114
Construction Administration (CA) phase, 43, 46
Construction Documentation (CD) phase, 43, 45–46
construction workers, 93
COVID-19 pandemic, 13
craft: Braverman on, 32; professionalism versus, 42; Socrates on, 53; tekhnē and, 54
creative consciousness, 61–68, 88
creativity, 48–54, 84; commodification of, 70; Lukács on, 66–68; mystification of, 54–61; as passive and active force, 65–66
credentialism, 64–65, 69
cult of creativity, 67
cultural production, 140–43

Daston, Lorraine, 123
Deamer, Peggy, 41
Descartes, René, 123, 125
design, 17; construction divided from, 23; creativity and, 48–54; ethics of, 59–60;

expanded notion of, 109; as exploitation, 68–75; history of, 22; phases of, 42–47; professionalization of, 63–64; specialization within, 76–83
design-based education, 58
design capital, 74
Design Development (DD) phase, 43, 45
designers: exploitation of, 60; Lukács on status of, 68; as petty-bourgeoisie, 90; status of, 84–86
Design Knowledge (DK), 126–27
design studios, 55–57
design workers, 67, 70–72, 79–80
development, 130–31
dialogical learning mode, 55
drafting, 97
Du Bois, W. E. B., 109, 119–21, 145

ecological theory, 123
ecology, 112, 123, 134–35
Electric Vehicles (EV), 105
environmental crisis, 122
ethics of design, 59–60
exploitation: design as, 68–75; of designers, 60; Du Bois on, 120; Parkin on credentialism and, 64; Poulantzas on, 80; Erik Olin Wright on, 87, 90

factory system, 28
facts, 123–24
Fain, Shawn, 104, 121
false consciousness, 68
feminism, 116–18
fictitious commodities, 29
fine arts, 60
Florida, Richard, 78
Foster, John Bellemy, 112, 127, 133–35
Franklin, Samuel Weil, 51–54, 64
Fraser, Nancy, 116; on class, 15–16; on distinction between labor and capital, 29–30; on gender and labor, 112–14; on race, 121; on transformative movements, 122
Freire, Paulo, 55

Gago, Veronica, 70, 116–19, 122
gender, 113–15
Ghosh, Amitav, 124, 126, 136
Gothic architecture, 23
graphic designers, 107, 111

Harvey, David, 140–41
heating of buildings, 130–31, 136–37
hooks, bell, 131, 133
Howard, Robert, 99–101
Hurricane Katrina, 128
Hurricane Sandy, 129

INDEX

identity politics, 114, 122
Ingold, Tim, 50–51
innovation in production, 103–4
internal labor markets, 72–73
International Association of Machinists and Aerospace Workers (IAM), 34, 36
iPhones, 51, 74

Jacobs, Jane, 115

Kimmerer, Robin Wall, 125, 135

labor: productive and unproductive, 74–75; unpaid, 116
land, Du Bois on, 120
Lanier, Jaron, 101
Latrobe, Benjamin Henry, 25
Lefebvre, Henri, 51, 78, 140
Le Guin, Ursula K., 110
L'Enfant, Pierre, 25–26
Leonardo da Vinci, 24
Los Angeles (California), 137
Lukács, Georg, 65–68, 88–91

Malm, Andreas, 136
Marx, Karl, 13–15, 24, 91, 109; on architects, 77; on "commodity-structure," 66; on exploitation, 90–91; on factory system, 28; on "material intelligence," 50; on metabolic rift, 13, 127, 131, 133–34; on middle class fractions, 85–86; on petty-bourgeoisie, 89; on planning process, 49; on surplus-value, 69–70; on technology, 136
Maslow, Abraham H., 82
material intelligence, 49–50
Matrix (architectural collective), 114–16, 119, 122
McAlevey, Jane, 39
McGhee, Heather, 121–22
medicine, 50
metabolic rift, 127–29, 131–34
midcentury modernism, 115
Mills, C. Wright, 79–80
Milwaukee (Wisconsin), 145
Mobile (Alabama), 121–22
modernism, 115
Morris, William, 30–31, 91–92, 95, 139

Native Americans, 87
nature, 124–25
New Orleans (Louisiana), 128–29
The New School, 105
New York City (New York), 138, 140
Ni Una Menos (Not One More; Argentinean movement), 116, 117, 121

office workers, 58

Panopticon, 28

Parkin, Frank, 63, 64
Passive House standards, 137
petty-bourgeoisie, 87, 89; designers as, 90; Du Bois on, 120
Plato, 19, 53–54
Polanyi, Karl, 27–29, 141
Polanyi, Michael, 107–9
Poulantzas, Nicos, 80, 81
praxis, 122–23
productive labor, 74–75
productivity, 104, 116
professionalism, 84; craft versus, 42
professionalization, 63
publishing industry, unionization of, 142–43

racism, 122
Reagan, Ronald, 145
real estate, stock market crash of 2008 and, 11–12
Reconstruction era (U.S.), 119, 121
Renaissance, 22–23

Schematic Design (SD) phase, 43–45
Scientific Ecological Knowledge (SEK), 123, 125–27, 135
Shiva, Vandana, 129–31
SHoP architects (firm), 34
skilled workers, 87
sociology, 112, 134
Socrates, 19, 53, 65

software, used in architecture, 94–95
Sophists, 53
status, 62–63, 68; of designers, 84–85, 89
status consciousness, 65, 68
status groups, 62–63
Steinbeck, John, 14
Stewart, Matthew, 78–79
Stone, Harris, 20–21
strikes: feminist, 117–18; of writers and actors, 96, 98, 106–7
strollers, 115–16
student debt, 70, 73
styles of life, 62–63
surplus-value, 69–70, 75

Tafuri, Manfredo, 21, 40–41
Táíwò, Olúfẹ́mi O., 129, 143
technology: artificial intelligence and, 106–7; Marx on, 136; software used in architecture, 94–98; UTOPIA Project on development of, 99–101
tekhnē (craft), 53–54, 67, 69
Tennessee Valley Authority (TVA), 143–45
Thompson, E. P., 30, 31, 141–43
Traditional Ecological Knowledge (TEK), 123, 125–27, 135
transformation, 114
transversality, 117

unionization, 19–20; at Bernheimer Architecture, 35–39; credentialism versus, 64; of cultural workers, 142; in design industries, 86; at SHoP architects, 34; by UAW, 104–5; at universities, 80

unions: effects of new technology studied by, 99–100; Gago on, 117; United Auto Workers, 104–6; Yates on, 142–43

United Auto Workers (UAW), 104–6

unpaid labor, 116

unproductive labor, 74–75

Upjohn, Richard, 81

UTOPIA Project (Sweden), 99–101

video game workers, 96, 107

Vitruvian Man (painting, Leonardo da Vinci), 24

Vitruvius, 23–25

Volvo (firm), 102

Wank, Roland A., 144

Weber, Max, 62–63, 68, 89, 90

white labor, 120

women, 111, 115–16

Woods, Mary N., 17, 25–26, 28

work, Morris on, 91

workers: definitions of, 117; Du Bois on, 119–20

work hours, 71

Wright, Erik Olin, 88; on classes under capitalism, 87; on exploitation, 72, 75, 90–91

Wright, Frank Lloyd, 10

writers, strike by, 96, 98, 106–7

Writers Guild of America (WGA), 106

Yates, Michael, 142–43

www.ingramcontent.com/pod-product-compliance
Ingram Content Group UK Ltd.
Pitfield, Milton Keynes, MK11 3LW, UK
UKHW010850171125
465146UK00003B/80